The Sasanian Empire

The Rise and Fall of Ancient Persia's Last Great Dynasty

Samuel Corwin

Table of Contents

Introduction: Why the Sasanian Empire Matters........................1

Part 1: Origins and Rise..9

Chapter 1: Before the Sasanians - A Fractured Iran.................10

Chapter 2: Ardashir I and the Birth of Empire....................18

Chapter 3: Inventing a New Persia................................28

Part 2: Building the Imperial Machine.........................37

Chapter 4: The King of Kings.....................................38

Chapter 5: The Machinery of Empire...............................48

Chapter 6: Law, Order, and the Governed Empire...................57

Part 3 Religion, Society, and Power...........................67

Chapter 7: Fire and Faith - Zoroastrianism as State Power........68

Chapter 8: A World of Many Faiths................................78

Chapter 9: Life in the Empire....................................87

Chapter 10: Women and Gender in the Sasanian World...............97

Part 4: War, Diplomacy, and Global Power.....................107

Chapter 11: Rome vs. Persia - The Endless War....................108

Chapter 12: The Sasanian War Machine.............................117

Chapter 13: A World of Rivals and Allies - Sasanian Diplomacy 125

Part 5: Culture and Civilization.............................135

Chapter 14: Wealth of an Empire..................................136

Chapter 15: Cities of Power......................................147

Chapter 16: Art of Empire..157

Chapter 17: Luxury and Identity 166

Chapter 18: Minds of the Empire - Science, Medicine, and Learning..176

Part 6: Crisis, Collapse, and Legacy 185

Chapter 19: Cracks in the System 186

Chapter 20: Revolution and Reform - The Mazdakite Crisis........ 194

Chapter 21: The Final Collapse.. 204

Chapter 22: The Empire That Never Truly Died........................... 213

Conclusion: Legacy of a Forgotten Superpower 222

A Note on Sources 231

Introduction:
Why the Sasanian Empire Matters

The Sasanian Empire at Its Height (c. 620 CE)

Between Rome and Islam stood a superpower that most people have never heard of.

For more than four centuries - from 224 AD to 651 AD - the Sasanian Empire dominated the ancient world's eastern half. It fought Rome to a standstill across generations of brutal warfare. It produced art, architecture, and philosophy that would echo through Byzantine cathedrals and Islamic palaces alike. Its kings called themselves "King of Kings," and they meant it. Yet ask most educated readers today to name a Sasanian emperor, describe a Sasanian city, or explain what the empire believed, and you will likely be met with silence.

That silence is the problem this book sets out to fix.

The Sasanians ruled what they called *Ērānshahr* - "the realm of the Iranians" - a vast stretch of territory running from modern Iraq to Afghanistan, from the Caucasus mountains to the Persian Gulf. At its height, this was one of the most powerful states on earth, a peer rival to Rome and later Byzantium, a sophisticated civilization with a state religion, a professional army, a complex bureaucracy, and a royal court of legendary splendor. And yet, compared to Rome or Greece or even the earlier Achaemenid Persians, the Sasanians remain curiously absent from popular history.

The Invisible Empire in History

Part of the problem is geography. The Sasanian heartland sits in what is today Iran and Iraq, regions that Western readers often encounter only through the lens of modern politics or ancient biblical history. The great Sasanian cities - Ctesiphon, Gundeshapur, Bishapur - don't appear on the mental maps most of us carry. Their ruins don't draw the same tourist traffic as the Colosseum or the Parthenon. Their names don't roll off the tongue with the easy familiarity of Caesar or Alexander.

Part of the problem is also timing. The Sasanians fall into an awkward historical gap. They come after the Achaemenid Persians, who are famous for fighting the Greeks at Marathon and Thermopylae, and after the Parthians, who are at least known as Rome's eastern nemesis. They end with the Islamic conquests of the seventh century - a transformation so dramatic that it tends to swallow everything that came before it. The Sasanians are sandwiched between more famous stories, and they suffer for it.

Then there is the question of sources. Unlike Rome, which produced an enormous literary tradition in Latin that European scholars have studied continuously for centuries, the Sasanian Empire left behind relatively few written records in its own language. Middle Persian - the language of the Sasanian court - was not widely studied in Western universities until the modern era. Much of what we know about the Sasanians comes filtered through Roman historians, Armenian chronicles, or later Islamic sources, each carrying their own biases and blind spots.

This is not a small irony. One of the most powerful empires of late antiquity has been largely reconstructed through the eyes of its enemies and successors.

Not Just Rome's Rival

It would be easy - and wrong - to define the Sasanian Empire purely in terms of its relationship with Rome. Yes, the two empires fought each other with remarkable persistence across centuries of conflict. Yes, the struggle for control of Mesopotamia, Armenia, and the Syrian frontier shaped both powers in profound ways. But reducing the Sasanians to "Rome's eastern rival" is like describing the Byzantine Empire as merely "the eastern half of Rome." It captures something real while missing almost everything that matters.

The Sasanian Empire was a civilization in its own right, with its own internal logic, its own cultural achievements, and its own vision of what an empire should be.

Ardashir I, who founded the dynasty in 224 AD by overthrowing the last Parthian king, was not simply a warlord seizing power. He was a political architect. Under his rule and that of his successors, the Sasanians built a centralized administrative system that transformed a patchwork of regional kingdoms into a coherent imperial state. They elevated Zoroastrianism - one of the world's oldest monotheistic traditions - into a state religion, creating a powerful alliance between the royal court and the Zoroastrian priesthood that would define Persian identity for centuries.

Militarily, the Sasanians were formidable innovators. Their heavily armored cavalry, the *savaran*, represented some of the most sophisticated mounted warfare of the ancient world. Kings like Khosrow implemented military reforms that kept the empire competitive against both Roman legions and the nomadic peoples pressing from the north and east. At the Battle of Bukhara, Sasanian forces allied with the Western Turkic Khaganate to confront the Hephthalite Empire - a reminder that Sasanian strategic thinking extended far beyond the Roman frontier, reaching deep into Central Asia.

Culturally, the Sasanian court became a center of intellectual exchange that historians are only beginning to appreciate fully. Greek philosophical texts were translated into Middle Persian. Indian mathematical and astronomical knowledge flowed westward through Sasanian intermediaries. The royal city of Ctesiphon, near modern Baghdad, was one of the largest cities in the world during the empire's peak. When the Arab armies finally swept through in the 640s and 650s, they did not conquer a decaying relic - they conquered a living civilization.

Why the Sasanians Still Matter Today

The fall of the Sasanian Empire in 651 AD did not erase its influence. It transmitted it.

Much of what we think of as distinctly "Islamic" in art, architecture, and court culture has deep Sasanian roots. The domed palace architecture that became a hallmark of Islamic civilization drew heavily on Sasanian models. Persian administrative traditions - the language of bureaucracy, the structures of provincial governance - were absorbed wholesale into the early Islamic caliphates. The very concept of the divinely sanctioned, absolute monarch that shaped Islamic political thought owed an enormous debt to Sasanian kingship ideology.

Even further west, the Sasanian legacy shaped Byzantium. Centuries of warfare and diplomatic contact left both empires permanently marked by each other. Byzantine court ceremonial, artistic motifs, and military organization all bear traces of Persian influence. The silk trade, the diplomatic marriages, the exchange of scholars and craftsmen - these were not incidental features of the Sasanian-Roman relationship. They were its substance.

For modern Iran, the Sasanian period carries particular weight. The empire's name for itself - *Ērānshahr*, the realm of the Iranians - is the direct ancestor of the word "Iran." Sasanian kings like Yazdgard I, remembered in tradition for his legendary hunting prowess, became figures of national mythology. The dynasty's championing of Zoroastrianism left a spiritual and cultural inheritance that persists in Iranian identity to this day, even after fourteen centuries of Islam.

To understand the medieval Islamic world, the Byzantine Empire, or modern Iran, you need to understand the Sasanians. There is no shortcut around them.

The Problem of Sources: How We Reconstruct Their World

Reconstructing the Sasanian Empire is genuinely difficult work, and any honest account of the period has to acknowledge that difficulty.

The Sasanians did not leave behind a Livy or a Thucydides - no great historian writing in Middle Persian whose works survived intact into the modern era. The royal inscriptions that do survive, carved into cliffsides and stone monuments, tell us something about how kings

5

wished to be remembered, but they are not narrative history. They are propaganda, carefully crafted and selectively truthful.

Much of our written evidence comes from outsiders. Roman and Byzantine historians wrote about the Sasanians extensively, but always from the perspective of a rival power - one that alternately feared, admired, and despised its Persian neighbor. Armenian sources offer a different angle, particularly on the religious and political conflicts of the frontier zones, but Armenian writers had their own agendas and loyalties. Later Islamic historians, writing in Arabic and Persian after the conquest, preserved fragments of Sasanian tradition but also reshaped them to fit new religious and political frameworks.

Archaeology fills some of the gaps. Excavations at Sasanian sites have uncovered palace complexes, fire temples, coins, seals, and luxury goods that paint a vivid picture of material culture. Rock reliefs - monumental carvings depicting royal hunts, military victories, and divine investitures - survive at sites like Naqsh-e Rostam and Taq-e Bostan, offering direct visual evidence of how Sasanian kings presented themselves to the world.

Scholars differ on how to weigh these different types of evidence, and on how much certainty is possible when reconstructing a civilization this distant and this incompletely documented. What follows in this book is built on the best available scholarship, presented as clearly as the evidence allows - and with honesty about where the evidence runs thin.

How to Read This Book - and This Series

This book is not a comprehensive academic history of the Sasanian Empire. It does not attempt to resolve every scholarly debate or survey every corner of a four-century empire. What it does attempt is something arguably more important for most readers: to make the Sasanians real.

Real in the sense of human. Real in the sense of consequential. Real in the sense that their choices, their conflicts, and their achievements shaped a world that we still, in many ways, inhabit.

Each chapter that follows focuses on a specific dimension of Sasanian civilization - its founding and political structure, its wars and diplomacy, its religion and culture, its economy and society, and finally its fall and afterlife. The goal is not to overwhelm with detail but to build, piece by piece, a portrait of an empire that deserves to be known.

A few things to keep in mind as you read. First, names and dates in this period can be slippery. Different sources transliterate Middle Persian names differently, and ancient chronologies don't always align perfectly with modern scholarship. Where there is genuine uncertainty, this book says so rather than papering over it with false confidence.

Second, the Sasanian Empire was not a monolith. It changed dramatically over four centuries, and the empire of Ardashir I in the 220s looked very different from the empire that collapsed before the Arab armies in the 650s. Resist the temptation to treat it as a static entity.

Third - and perhaps most importantly - try to encounter the Sasanians on their own terms before measuring them against Rome or Islam. They were not a prelude to something else. They were a civilization complete in themselves, with their own internal drama, their own moments of greatness and failure, their own ways of making sense of the world.

That civilization is what this book is about.

Quick Summary

- The Sasanian Empire lasted from 224 AD to 651 AD, making it one of late antiquity's most durable powers.

- Founded by Ardashir I, the empire built a centralized state, elevated Zoroastrianism as its official religion, and developed sophisticated military and administrative systems.

- The Sasanians were not simply Rome's rival - they were a major civilization whose influence extended from Central Asia to the Mediterranean world.

- Their cultural and administrative legacy was absorbed by both the early Islamic caliphates and the Byzantine Empire, shaping the medieval world in ways that remain underappreciated.

- Reconstructing Sasanian history is challenging because most surviving sources come from outsiders - Roman, Armenian, and Islamic writers - rather than from Sasanian voices themselves.

- Archaeology, royal inscriptions, and material culture help fill the gaps left by the literary record.

- Understanding the Sasanians is essential for anyone who wants to grasp the roots of Islamic civilization, Byzantine culture, or Iranian national identity.

Four centuries is a long time. Empires that last four centuries leave marks that don't disappear when the last king falls. The Sasanian Empire ended in 651 AD, but its ideas, its art, its administrative genius, and its vision of Persian kingship flowed forward into everything that came after. What follows is the story of how that empire was built, how it functioned, how it fought, and why - even now - it refuses to stay forgotten.

Part 1
Origins and Rise

Chapter 1:
Before the Sasanians - A Fractured Iran

Empires rarely emerge from nothing. They rise from the ruins of what came before, from the exhaustion, the contradictions, and the slow-burning failures of the system they replace. To understand the Sasanian Empire, one of the ancient world's most formidable and enduring powers, you first have to understand the world it shattered: the Parthian order, a civilization that lasted nearly five centuries and yet, in the end, could not hold itself together.

The Arsacid dynasty ruled over a vast stretch of the ancient world from roughly 247 BCE to 224 CE. At its greatest extent, the Parthian Empire reached from eastern Turkey in the west to the borders of what is now Afghanistan in the east. By any measure, it was an enormous political achievement. But size and coherence are different things entirely. The system the Arsacids built was not a monolithic state. It was a patchwork - a confederation of noble families, regional strongmen, and semi-autonomous kingdoms held together by a mixture of loyalty, self-interest, and the occasional threat of force. When that mixture worked, it produced stability. When it didn't, it produced something far more dangerous: an empire that looked whole from the outside but was fracturing from within.

By the early third century CE, the fractures had become impossible to ignore. Royal authority had eroded to near-irrelevance. Noble clans operated as independent powers in all but name. Trade revenues were declining, the western frontier with Rome bled men and money, and succession to the throne had become less a matter of dynastic right than aristocratic bargaining. The Parthian world was not collapsing in a single dramatic event. It was unraveling, thread by thread, and that unraveling created the conditions in which a determined challenger from the old Persian heartland could seize everything.

The Parthian System: Power Without Unity

For almost five hundred years, the Arsacid dynasty maintained its grip on one of the ancient world's largest empires. The method they chose was not rigid centralization but accommodation. Rather than dismantling the local power structures they encountered as they expanded, the Arsacids absorbed them. Kings, nobles, clan chiefs, and regional strongmen were permitted to retain their titles, their lands, and much of their authority, provided they acknowledged Arsacid supremacy and supplied soldiers when called upon. The result was less an empire in the Roman sense and more a vast, loosely stitched confederation of semi-autonomous territories, each with its own loyalties, its own traditions, and its own ambitions.

This arrangement had real advantages, especially in the early centuries. It made conquest faster and administration cheaper. A dynasty that did not need to govern every corner of its territory directly did not need the enormous bureaucratic machinery that true centralization demands. Local rulers handled local problems. The Arsacid king sat at the top of the hierarchy, but the hierarchy itself was wide, shallow, and full of gaps.

What made the system work in times of strength made it dangerous in times of stress.

When a capable king sat on the throne and commanded genuine loyalty, the feudal lords fell into line. But when the center weakened, as it periodically did, those same lords became a source of instability. Succession disputes were chronic. The Parthian nobility did not merely witness royal transitions; they actively shaped them, backing rival claimants, switching allegiances, and occasionally deposing kings who failed to satisfy their interests. Power, in the Parthian world, was always being negotiated.

This was not simply a flaw in Arsacid character or ambition. It was structural. A system built on distributed authority cannot easily reclaim that authority when it needs to. The very lords who made the empire governable in peacetime became its most dangerous internal opponents in crisis. And crises, in the ancient world, were never far away.

A Land of Kings and Clans

To picture Parthian Iran as a single, unified country would be to misread it fundamentally. What the Arsacids ruled was better understood as a web of competing power centers - great noble families whose roots ran deep into the Iranian plateau and whose influence over their own territories was, in practical terms, nearly absolute.

Several of these aristocratic clans were genuinely ancient, their prestige predating the Arsacids themselves. Families like the Suren and the Karen held hereditary rights and privileges that no king could easily revoke. They commanded their own armies, administered their own estates, and maintained their own courts. In some respects, they functioned less like subjects of the Arsacid king and more like junior partners in a shared enterprise - partners who expected to be consulted, compensated, and respected.

This clan-based structure gave Iranian society a particular texture. Loyalty was intensely personal and local before it was imperial or abstract. A soldier fought for his lord. A lord answered to the king - but only so long as the king remained powerful enough to demand it. When that power faltered, the web of obligation unraveled quickly.

The implications for military organization were significant. Parthian armies were not standing professional forces in the way that Rome's legions were. They were assembled from the retinues of noble houses, brought together for specific campaigns and then dispersed again. The famous Parthian cavalry - the heavily armored cataphracts and the swift horse archers who could loose arrows while riding at full gallop - were expressions of aristocratic military culture as much as they were tactical innovations. A great lord's worth was measured, in part, by the quality of the horsemen he could put in the field.

This produced warriors of genuine skill and ferocity. It did not produce an army that could be reliably mobilized, consistently supplied, or easily commanded across long distances. When the Parthians fought Rome, they could achieve spectacular results - the catastrophic Roman defeat at Carrhae in 53 BCE, where the general Crassus lost his life and his legions, remains one of the most stunning military upsets of the ancient world. But sustaining campaigns, holding conquered territory, and projecting power over time required a different kind of institutional strength than the Parthians possessed.

Iran's geography reinforced these divisions. Mountain ranges, deserts, and river valleys create natural barriers between regions, making communication slow and central control difficult. Communities separated by the Zagros Mountains or the great central desert developed distinct identities and interests. The Arsacids could claim sovereignty over all of it. Exercising that sovereignty uniformly was another matter.

Rome on the Western Frontier

No account of Parthian weakness can ignore the pressure that came from the west. For much of the Arsacid period, Rome and Parthia faced each other across a contested frontier in Mesopotamia and the Levant, and the relationship between the two empires shaped both of them in ways that neither fully controlled.

At times the rivalry produced open war. Rome's ambitions in the east were persistent and often aggressive. Several Roman commanders - Crassus, Mark Antony, Trajan - launched major campaigns against Parthia, with results that ranged from catastrophic defeat to temporary conquest. Trajan, in the early second century CE, pushed deep into Parthian territory and briefly captured Ctesiphon, the Arsacid capital on the Tigris. But Roman gains in the east proved difficult to hold, and the frontier eventually stabilized along lines that neither side found entirely satisfactory.

What the Roman wars cost the Parthians was not just territory or soldiers. They cost legitimacy. A king who could not defend his borders, who watched Roman armies march through his heartland, who lost his capital - even temporarily - faced questions about his fitness to rule that the noble clans were quick to exploit. Military failure fed political instability, and political instability invited further military failure. The Arsacids never fully broke that cycle.

The western frontier also consumed resources that the empire could ill afford. Maintaining armies, fortifying cities, and rewarding loyal lords in the border regions placed constant financial demands on the Arsacid treasury. The Parthians controlled significant trade routes - the overland paths that connected the Mediterranean world to Central Asia and beyond - and the revenues from that commerce were vital. But trade income was variable, and the costs of frontier defense were not.

Rome was not the only external pressure. The eastern frontier presented its own challenges, as nomadic peoples and rival powers in Central Asia periodically tested Parthian strength. The empire was, in a real sense, always fighting on multiple fronts - and doing so with a military and administrative system that was not built for sustained, simultaneous pressure.

Economic and Political Weaknesses

Beneath the military strains lay structural economic problems that compounded over time. The Parthian economy rested heavily on its position as a middleman in long-distance trade. Goods moving between the Roman Empire and the markets of India and China passed through Parthian territory, and the tolls and taxes levied on that commerce generated substantial revenue for the Arsacid court and the noble families who controlled key routes.

But this dependence on transit trade created a particular kind of vulnerability. When trade volumes fell - because of war, disruption, or the gradual development of alternative sea routes - the revenues that sustained the Parthian system fell with them. Unlike empires with deep agricultural bases and sophisticated tax bureaucracies, the Arsacids lacked the institutional machinery to extract consistent revenue from their own population. The decentralized structure that made the empire governable also made it fiscally fragile. Local lords collected local revenues. How much of that wealth flowed upward to the center depended on loyalty and negotiation, not law and enforcement.

Political instability made everything worse. The Arsacid succession was never regularized in a way that prevented conflict. When a king died - or was killed - the great noble families convened to select or confirm his successor, and that process was rarely smooth. Rival claimants emerged. Factions formed. Civil wars erupted. In the final century of Arsacid rule, the throne changed hands with alarming frequency, and each transition left the dynasty weaker and the nobility more powerful.

By the early third century CE, the Arsacid king was less an absolute monarch than a first among competing magnates - a figure whose authority depended on constant management of aristocratic interests rather than genuine command. The empire still existed. But the coherence that makes an empire more than a geographic expression had largely dissolved.

Why Change Was Inevitable

Looking back, it is tempting to see the fall of the Parthians as inevitable - a slow-motion collapse that had been building for generations. That framing is too tidy. Empires can persist in dysfunction for a very long time, and the Arsacids had survived crises before. What made the early third century different was not simply accumulated weakness but the emergence of a specific challenger with the will, the ideology, and the military capacity to exploit that weakness.

That challenger came from Persis, the ancient heartland of the earlier Achaemenid Persian Empire, in what is now the Fars province of southern Iran. The Sasanians - the family that would overthrow the Arsacids and build something genuinely new - drew on a deep well of Persian cultural and religious identity that the Arsacids, for all their longevity, had never fully claimed. Where the Parthians had been accommodating and syncretic, the Sasanians would be assertive and ideologically coherent. Where the Arsacids had distributed power, the Sasanians would work to concentrate it.

But that story belongs to the chapters ahead. What matters here is the foundation: a Parthian world that was, by the time of its end, exhausted by its own contradictions. A system of governance that had once been flexible enough to hold a vast empire together had become too fragmented to defend it. A dynasty that had once commanded genuine loyalty had become a prize to be captured rather than a source of order to be upheld.

Change, when it came, would not arrive as a surprise. It would arrive as a consequence.

Quick Summary

- The Parthian (Arsacid) Empire lasted from approximately 247 BCE to 224 CE, spanning a vast territory from eastern Turkey to Afghanistan.

- Arsacid rule was built on decentralized feudalism: local kings and noble clans retained significant autonomy in exchange for nominal loyalty to the Arsacid king.

- Powerful aristocratic families - some predating the Arsacids - controlled their own armies, lands, and courts, making true centralization impossible.

- Parthian military strength rested on noble cavalry retinues rather than professional standing armies, producing tactical brilliance but strategic inconsistency.

- Prolonged conflict with Rome on the western frontier drained Parthian resources, destabilized royal authority, and exposed the limits of the Arsacid system.

- The empire's economy depended heavily on transit trade revenues, leaving it financially vulnerable when those revenues declined.

- Chronic succession disputes empowered the nobility at the expense of the throne, and by the early third century CE, Arsacid authority had become more nominal than real.

- These structural weaknesses created the conditions in which a determined regional challenger - the Sasanians - could rise and succeed.

What the Parthians left behind was not simply a power vacuum. They left a template - of what an Iranian empire could be, and of what it could not afford to remain. The Sasanians would study that template carefully, and they would build something designed, from its very foundations, to correct every flaw they saw in it. Whether they succeeded, and at what cost, is the story that follows.

Chapter 2:
Ardashir I and the Birth of Empire

One man didn't just take power - he redefined what power meant. When Ardashir I rode out of the province of Fars in the early third century CE, he carried with him not just military ambition but a vision of empire so total, so deliberately constructed, that it would shape the Middle East for four centuries. He wasn't simply overthrowing a dynasty. He was erasing one world and building another from the foundations up.

The Weight of a New Beginning

Most empires are born in chaos and explained in hindsight. The Sasanian Empire is different. From its earliest days, it announced itself with intention - through coins, cities, monuments, and a religious ideology woven so tightly into the fabric of kingship that the two became nearly inseparable. Ardashir I understood something that many conquerors miss: winning battles is the easy part. Legitimacy is the real prize.

A regional strongman from a priestly family in southern Persia dismantled the four-century-old Parthian order, defeated its last king on a battlefield in 224 CE, and then spent the remaining years of his life constructing something that would outlast him by centuries. His story is one of personal ambition, yes - but also of ideology, memory, and the deliberate invocation of a glorious Persian past.

Understanding Ardashir means understanding what came before him, what he destroyed, and what he chose to build in its place. The Sasanian Empire didn't emerge from a vacuum. It emerged from a man who knew exactly what he wanted history to say about him.

Origins of Ardashir

Ardashir came from Fars - the ancient heartland of Persia, the same region that had given the world Cyrus the Great and the Achaemenid Empire centuries before. This was no accident of geography. It was a fact Ardashir would spend his entire reign exploiting.

His family background placed him at the intersection of two powerful institutions: the temple and the court. His grandfather, Sasan, was reportedly a priest associated with the fire temple at Istakhr, a site of deep religious significance in the Zoroastrian tradition. His father, Papak, was a local ruler who governed the district of Khir under the authority of the Parthian vassal king of Fars. Ardashir was thus born into a family that already straddled religious prestige and political power - a combination that would define his empire.

What exactly Ardashir's early life looked like is difficult to reconstruct with precision. Later Sasanian sources, eager to mythologize their founder, layered his biography with legend. But the broad outlines are credible: he grew up in an environment where Zoroastrian ritual and local governance were intertwined, where the memory of Achaemenid greatness was not a distant abstraction but a living cultural inheritance. Istakhr sat near the ruins of Persepolis. The carved reliefs of Achaemenid kings were visible from the roads Ardashir would have traveled as a young man.

His father Papak had himself been ambitious. Around 205 to 210 CE, Papak moved against the existing king of Fars and seized control of the region, installing himself as its ruler. When Papak died, a succession dispute broke out among his sons. Ardashir, who had been governing the district of Darabgird, moved quickly and decisively - eliminating his brother Shapur, who had been positioned as heir, and taking control of Fars for himself.

This early episode reveals something essential about Ardashir's character. He was not a man who waited for opportunity. He created it.

With Fars secured, he began expanding outward. He subdued neighboring districts - Kerman, Isfahan, and parts of what is now southwestern Iran - absorbing them into a growing personal domain. Each conquest was more than territorial. It was a statement. A regional lord was becoming something else entirely.

The Parthian king, Artabanus IV, watched this expansion with growing alarm. He reportedly summoned Ardashir and demanded he halt his campaigns. Ardashir refused. The confrontation that had been building for years was now inevitable.

Rebellion Against the Arsacids

To understand what Ardashir was rebelling against, it helps to understand what the Parthian Empire had become by the early third century CE.

The Arsacid dynasty, which had ruled Persia and Mesopotamia since roughly 247 BCE, had never been a monolithic centralized state. It functioned, in many ways, as a confederation - a network of semi-autonomous vassal kingdoms held together by the prestige of the Arsacid royal house, the threat of military force, and the economic benefits of controlling the Silk Road trade routes between Rome and China. At its height, this system worked. By the early third century, it was fraying badly.

Rome had been a persistent and punishing adversary. The campaigns of Trajan in the early second century CE had briefly pushed Roman power deep into Mesopotamia, and while the Parthians recovered, the wars left scars - political, economic, and psychological. The reign of Artabanus IV himself was shadowed by a Roman invasion under Caracalla in 216 CE, which sacked several Parthian cities and extracted a humiliating peace settlement. The Arsacid dynasty had also suffered from prolonged internal dynastic conflict, with Artabanus IV spending years fighting his own brother, Vologases VI, for control of the throne. By the time Ardashir began his rise, the Parthian Empire was not a colossus waiting to be toppled. It was a structure already cracking under its own weight.

Ardashir's rebellion was not spontaneous. It was methodical. After consolidating Fars and the surrounding regions, he moved against Parthian-aligned rulers in neighboring territories, defeating them one by one. Each victory expanded his resource base and his reputation. Each defeated vassal king sent a message to the others: the balance of power in Persia was shifting.

Artabanus IV responded by sending armies against Ardashir on at least two occasions before the final confrontation. Both times, Ardashir's forces prevailed. These early victories were militarily significant, but they were also deeply symbolic. Ardashir was not just winning battles - he was demonstrating that the Arsacid military machine, once feared across the ancient world, could be beaten.

What made Ardashir's rebellion so effective was its combination of military capability and ideological clarity. He wasn't presenting himself merely as a stronger warlord. He was presenting himself as a restorer - a man who would return Persia to the greatness it had known under the Achaemenids, a greatness that the Parthians, in his telling, had never truly embodied. The Arsacids were of Central Asian origin, Parthian nomads who had conquered Persia from the outside. Ardashir, by contrast, was from Fars itself, from the ancient Persian heartland. He understood the power of that distinction and used it relentlessly.

The Fall of the Parthians

The decisive moment came in 224 CE, at a place called Hormozdgan.

The exact location of the battle remains a matter of historical debate, but its outcome does not. Ardashir met Artabanus IV on the field, and the last Arsacid king of kings was killed. With Artabanus dead, the Parthian Empire - four centuries of Arsacid rule - effectively ceased to exist.

Consider what that moment represented. The Arsacid dynasty had survived Roman invasions, internal civil wars, and the rise and fall of countless regional powers. It had outlasted the Seleucid Empire that preceded it and had held its own against the might of Rome for generations. And yet it fell not to a foreign conqueror but to one of its own vassals, a man from a priestly family in the Persian south who had spent perhaps a decade methodically dismantling the empire's foundations before delivering the killing blow.

Ardashir's victory at Hormozdgan was not the end of resistance. Several Arsacid princes and their supporters continued to fight for years afterward, and pockets of Parthian-aligned power persisted in various regions. But the political reality had fundamentally changed. There was a new king of kings, and his name was Ardashir.

His treatment of the Arsacid legacy was revealing. Rather than simply erasing the Parthians from memory, Ardashir positioned his own dynasty as their rightful successors - and, more importantly, as the successors to something far older and grander. He looked past the Arsacids entirely, reaching back to the Achaemenids, to Cyrus and Darius, to the first Persian Empire that had stretched from the Aegean to the Indus. The Sasanian dynasty, in its own telling, was not a new beginning. It was a restoration.

This was sophisticated political theater, and it worked. By invoking the Achaemenid legacy, Ardashir gave his empire a sense of historical depth and legitimacy that no military victory alone could provide. He was not a usurper. He was a fulfillment.

Early Campaigns and Consolidation

Victory at Hormozdgan gave Ardashir the title of king of kings, but it did not give him a fully functioning empire. That had to be built - through further campaigns, administrative decisions, and the careful management of powerful regional interests.

In the years following 224 CE, Ardashir moved to consolidate control over territories that had been part of the Parthian sphere. Khuzestan, the fertile lowland region northeast of the Persian Gulf, was brought under direct Sasanian authority. Kerman, which Ardashir had already subdued during his earlier expansion, was integrated more firmly into the new imperial structure. Campaigns pushed into other regions as well, extending Sasanian influence and testing the boundaries of what the new empire could hold.

These were not easy conquests. Several regional rulers who had accepted Parthian overlordship were not automatically willing to accept Ardashir's. Some had to be defeated militarily; others were absorbed through negotiation or the strategic deployment of Sasanian prestige. The process was messy, as all real empire-building is.

Ardashir also turned his attention westward, toward Mesopotamia and the Roman frontier. Competition between Persia and Rome over the fertile crescent and the buffer kingdoms between them had defined the relationship for centuries. Ardashir launched campaigns against Roman-held territories, though the results were mixed. He was not yet in a position to fundamentally alter the balance with Rome - that would be the work of his son Shapur I - but he established the aggressive posture toward the west that would define Sasanian foreign policy for generations.

At home, Ardashir built the administrative and symbolic infrastructure of empire. He founded new cities - a practice with deep roots in Persian and Hellenistic tradition - and minted coins bearing his own image and titles. Those coins are among the most direct evidence we have of how Ardashir wanted to be seen: as a great king, a warrior, and a figure of divine favor.

Founding a New Order

Perhaps the most consequential thing Ardashir built was not a city or a military structure. It was a system of meaning.

Under the Parthians, religious life in Persia had been relatively decentralized. Zoroastrianism existed alongside other traditions, and the Arsacid kings, while not hostile to Zoroastrian practice, had not made it the defining ideology of their rule. Ardashir changed this. He placed Zoroastrianism - and specifically its fire cult, with its sacred flames and priestly hierarchies - at the center of Sasanian imperial identity.

This was not simply personal piety, though Ardashir's family background in the priestly class at Istakhr suggests genuine religious commitment. It was also political strategy of the highest order. By fusing royal authority with religious legitimacy, Ardashir created a system in which challenging the king meant, in some sense, challenging the divine order itself. The king was not merely a powerful man. He was the earthly representative of a cosmic truth.

This fusion of political power and religious ideology would become the defining characteristic of the Sasanian state. It gave the empire a coherence and an ideological resilience that the more loosely organized Parthian confederation had lacked. It also created tensions, particularly with religious minorities within the empire's borders, that would recur throughout Sasanian history.

Ardashir died in 241 CE, leaving the throne to his son Shapur I. By that point, the essential architecture of the Sasanian Empire was in place: a centralized monarchy claiming descent from the Achaemenids, a state religion that legitimized royal power, a professional military capable of challenging Rome, and a set of administrative practices that would govern one of the ancient world's great empires for the next four centuries.

Key Figures at a Glance

- **Ardashir I** - Founder of the Sasanian Empire. Rose from a priestly and administrative family in Fars to defeat the last Parthian king and establish a new imperial order. Reigned from 224 to 241 CE.

- **Artabanus IV** - Last king of kings of the Parthian Arsacid dynasty. Killed at the Battle of Hormozdgan in 224 CE. His death marked the end of nearly four centuries of Arsacid rule.

- **Shapur I** - Son and successor of Ardashir I. Became king of kings in 241 CE and extended the Sasanian Empire's power, most famously through dramatic victories against Rome.

- **Papak** - Ardashir's father. A local ruler in Fars who seized control of the region from its Parthian-appointed king, laying the groundwork for his son's far larger ambitions.

Legacy and Long-Term Impact

Ardashir I's achievement was not simply military. Plenty of men in the ancient world won battles and built short-lived kingdoms. What set Ardashir apart was his understanding that lasting power requires more than force - it requires a story.

By positioning the Sasanian dynasty as the heirs of the Achaemenids, he gave his empire a sense of historical purpose that transcended any individual reign. By fusing royal and religious authority, he created a governing ideology that proved remarkably durable. And by establishing the administrative and military foundations of the Sasanian state, he gave his successors the tools to build one of the ancient world's most sophisticated empires.

The Parthians had held Persia for four centuries, but they left behind relatively little in the way of cultural or institutional legacy. The Sasanians, by contrast, shaped Persian identity so profoundly that their influence can still be felt in Iranian culture, art, and religious tradition more than a thousand years after their empire fell.

Quick Summary

- Ardashir I came from Fars, the ancient Persian heartland, and from a family that combined priestly religious authority with local political power.

- His father Papak had already seized control of Fars before Ardashir expanded the family's power further, eliminating rivals and absorbing neighboring territories.

- The Parthian Empire was significantly weakened by Roman wars and internal dynastic conflict before Ardashir's rebellion began.

- At the Battle of Hormozdgan in 224 CE, Ardashir defeated and killed Artabanus IV, the last Arsacid king of kings, ending the Parthian Empire.

- Rather than simply replacing the Parthians, Ardashir claimed the legacy of the Achaemenids, positioning his dynasty as a restoration of ancient Persian greatness.

- He placed Zoroastrianism at the center of Sasanian imperial identity, fusing religious and political authority in ways that would define the empire for centuries.

- Ardashir founded cities, minted coins, and conducted campaigns to consolidate and expand his territory before his death in 241 CE.

- He left his son Shapur I an empire with solid ideological, administrative, and military foundations - the platform from which Sasanian power would reach its greatest heights.

What Ardashir built in those seventeen years between Hormozdgan and his death was, in the deepest sense, a framework for Persian identity - one that would survive conquests, religious transformations, and the passage of more than a millennium. His son Shapur would take that framework and test it against the greatest power in the western world. The results would astonish both empires.

Chapter 3:
Inventing a New Persia

Empires are not conquered. They are constructed.

The battlefield victory is only the beginning. Once the dust settles and the last rival king has been deposed, the harder work begins: persuading millions of people across dozens of cultures, languages, and traditions that they now belong to something larger than themselves. That they owe loyalty to a man they have never met, in a capital they may never see, who speaks a language they may not understand. This is the problem every empire-builder faces, and most fail at it long before any foreign army arrives at the gates.

Cyrus the Great solved this problem in ways that still astonish historians. Darius I refined the solution into something that would last for two centuries. Together, they did not merely conquer a territory. They invented a civilization.

Centralization Begins

When Cyrus overthrew the Median Empire in 550 BCE, he inherited not a blank slate but a patchwork. The ancient Near East was a mosaic of kingdoms, city-states, tribal confederacies, and priestly institutions, each with its own laws, gods, and expectations of power. Welding these pieces into a single functioning state required more than military force. It required a governing idea.

Cyrus's first instinct was to work *with* existing structures rather than against them. Where other conquerors dismantled local institutions and replaced them with their own, Cyrus largely left them intact. He allowed conquered peoples to keep their customs, practice their religions, and maintain their local hierarchies - provided they acknowledged Persian supremacy and paid their taxes. This was not weakness. It was a calculated strategy that dramatically reduced the cost of occupation.

What he built on top of these local foundations was something genuinely new: a centralized imperial administration capable of coordinating action across an enormous geographic space. At its core was the concept of the satrapy, a regional administrative unit governed by an appointed official called a satrap. The word itself derives from an Old Iranian term meaning "protector of the realm," and the role was precisely that: a representative of Persian royal authority embedded within a local context.

Satraps were not simply local governors left to their own devices. They collected taxes, maintained order, administered justice, and served as the king's eyes and ears in their territories. They commanded local military forces and bore responsibility for the security of their regions. But they operated within a framework set by the center, answerable to the king and subject to inspection by royal officials who traveled the empire's roads to ensure compliance.

This system was Cyrus's most durable invention. It acknowledged the reality of diversity while insisting on the fact of unity. A satrap in Egypt could govern according to Egyptian custom; a satrap in Lydia could respect Lydian tradition. Both answered to Persia. Both served the king. Both fed the same imperial machine.

The roads connecting these satrapies were not incidental - they were infrastructure as policy. Persian royal roads stretched thousands of miles across the empire, maintained at state expense and patrolled by royal couriers who could carry messages from one end of the empire to the other with remarkable speed. Trade followed these roads. So did armies. So did the king's authority.

Cyrus did not live to see his system fully mature. He died in battle in 530 BCE, leaving an empire that was vast but still consolidating. His son Cambyses extended Persian control into Egypt, adding yet another ancient civilization to the imperial portfolio. But it was Darius I who would take the administrative skeleton Cyrus had built and clothe it in muscle and sinew.

Crushing Regional Autonomy

Darius I came to power in 522 BCE under circumstances that were, to put it mildly, turbulent. A man named Gaumata had seized the throne, claiming to be Cambyses' murdered brother. Whether this was a genuine dynastic dispute or a priestly coup remains debated by historians. What is clear is that Darius - a member of a collateral branch of the Achaemenid line - overthrew Gaumata with the support of six Persian noble allies and then spent the better part of two years suppressing rebellions across virtually every corner of the empire.

The scale of the crisis was staggering. Babylon revolted. Egypt grew restless. Elam, Media, and several other provinces rose in open defiance. At one point, Darius was fighting on multiple fronts simultaneously, dispatching armies to different corners of his realm while personally leading campaigns elsewhere. His own account of this period, carved into the cliff face at Bisitun in western Iran, lists nineteen battles and the defeat of nine rebel kings in a single year. Even accounting for royal propaganda, the achievement was extraordinary.

What Darius understood - and what the rebellions had made brutally clear - was that the empire's diversity was also its vulnerability. Local elites left in place under Cyrus's tolerant model had retained enough power to challenge Persian authority when the center appeared weak. The satrap system, however elegant in theory, depended on the loyalty of men who commanded their own resources and their own soldiers.

Darius's response was to tighten the screws. He reorganized the satrapies, redrawing boundaries and reassigning governors to prevent any single official from accumulating too much independent power. He standardized taxation, establishing fixed tribute assessments for each province rather than leaving collection to local discretion. He created a class of royal inspectors - sometimes called "the king's eyes" - who traveled the empire conducting audits and reporting directly to the crown.

Military garrisons were stationed throughout the empire, not merely at its frontiers. Persian soldiers lived among the populations they oversaw, a constant physical reminder of where ultimate authority resided. Local rulers could keep their titles and their customs, but they could not keep their autonomy.

Darius also grasped that loyalty needed to be manufactured, not merely assumed. The Persian court became a theater of power, where satraps and tributary kings came to demonstrate their submission in person. Gifts were exchanged, honors were granted, and the hierarchy of the empire was performed in elaborate ritual. The famous relief carvings at Persepolis - Darius's great ceremonial capital - show delegations from across the empire bringing tribute to the Persian king, each group depicted in their distinctive dress, each carrying the products of their homeland. This was not merely art. It was a statement about how the world was ordered.

Building Loyalty and Control

Suppressing rebellion is one thing. Building genuine loyalty is another, and Darius pursued both with equal energy.

One of his most effective tools was the law. Darius presented his legal code as divinely ordained - not the arbitrary will of a king, but the expression of cosmic order as revealed through the Persian royal house. This framing was enormously powerful. It meant that obedience to Persian law was not merely political compliance; it was participation in a divinely sanctioned universe. To rebel against the king was not just treason. It was impiety.

Plato, writing centuries later, held Darius up as a model lawgiver, a ruler whose legal system had brought order and prosperity to an enormous realm. This was high praise from a Greek philosopher who had little reason to admire Persian kings. It suggests that Darius's reputation for just and consistent governance was not merely Persian self-promotion but something recognized even by his empire's rivals.

Beyond law, Darius invested heavily in the physical infrastructure of loyalty. The royal road system, begun under Cyrus, was expanded and formalized. Relay stations were established at regular intervals, staffed by royal couriers who could carry messages across the empire with a speed that astonished contemporaries. Herodotus, the Greek historian, famously described these couriers: "Neither snow nor rain nor heat nor gloom of night stays these couriers from the swift completion of their appointed rounds." The sentiment, later borrowed by the United States Postal Service, captures something real about the Persian system - a network of communication that made the empire feel, in some meaningful sense, connected.

Trade networks flourished along these same arteries. Persian standardization of weights, measures, and coinage made commerce across the empire more predictable and more profitable. Merchants moving goods from the Indus Valley to the Aegean coast could operate within a system of consistent rules. This was not altruism. It generated tax revenue and created constituencies of merchants and traders whose prosperity depended on Persian stability.

The Persian court itself served as a deliberate instrument of integration. Talented men from across the empire - Greeks, Babylonians, Egyptians, Lydians - found places in Persian service. The empire rewarded competence and loyalty regardless of ethnic origin. This was unusual in the ancient world, and it created a class of imperial servants whose careers and fortunes were tied to Persian success.

The Role of Religion in State Formation

Religion was never far from politics in the ancient world, and the Achaemenid kings understood this with particular clarity.

Cyrus had made religious toleration a cornerstone of his imperial policy. When he conquered Babylon in 539 BCE, he did not suppress the cult of Marduk, the city's patron deity - he participated in it. He presented himself as the chosen instrument of Marduk, the king who had come to restore proper worship after the impious reign of Nabonidus. By speaking the language of local religion, Cyrus transformed conquest into liberation. The Babylonians were not subjugated. They were rescued.

He applied the same logic elsewhere. His famous decree allowing the Jewish exiles in Babylon to return to their homeland and rebuild the Temple in Jerusalem is recorded in the Hebrew Bible, where Cyrus is described in terms of extraordinary reverence - as a shepherd chosen by God, even as a messiah. Whatever Cyrus's personal motivations, the political effect was clear: he had turned a potentially restive population into grateful subjects.

Darius built on this foundation but added a distinctly Persian theological dimension. He was a devoted worshipper of Ahura Mazda, the supreme deity of Zoroastrianism, and his inscriptions consistently attribute his victories and his authority to Ahura Mazda's favor. The Bisitun inscription opens with a declaration that Ahura Mazda made Darius king, that it was by Ahura Mazda's will that the rebellions were crushed, that the cosmic order - *asha*, truth and righteousness - had been restored through Persian arms.

This was more than personal piety. It was a theological claim about the nature of Persian rule. The king did not merely govern by force or by tradition. He governed because the supreme god of the universe had chosen him to do so. Resistance to Persian authority was therefore resistance to divine order itself.

Darius did not impose Zoroastrianism on his subjects. The policy of religious toleration that Cyrus had established remained in force. But the theological framing of Persian kingship gave the empire a spiritual backbone that purely administrative arrangements could not provide. The king was not just the most powerful man in the world. He was the earthly representative of cosmic truth.

The First Imperial Identity

What Cyrus and Darius built, across eight decades of conquest and consolidation, was something the ancient world had not quite seen before: an empire with a self-conscious identity.

Previous empires - Assyrian, Babylonian, Egyptian - had been centered on a single culture that dominated others. The Achaemenid Empire was different. It was explicitly multi-ethnic, multilingual, and multi-religious, yet it possessed a coherent Persian identity at its core. The king was Persian. The language of administration was Aramaic, a practical lingua franca, but the language of royal prestige was Old Persian. The art of Persepolis drew on Egyptian, Babylonian, Greek, and Lydian traditions simultaneously - a deliberate visual statement that Persia could absorb and transcend all of them.

This was the first imperial identity in the modern sense: not the erasure of difference, but its organization under a single sovereign framework. Subject peoples were not required to become Persian. They were required to acknowledge that Persia was the center around which everything else orbited.

That idea - the empire as a universal order, tolerant of diversity but insistent on hierarchy - would echo forward through centuries. Alexander the Great, when he conquered Persia in 330 BCE, did not simply destroy what he found. He tried to inherit it, adopting Persian court customs and presenting himself as the legitimate successor to the Achaemenid kings. That was perhaps the greatest testament to what Cyrus and Darius had built: an empire so well constructed that even its conqueror wanted to wear its crown.

Quick Summary

- Cyrus the Great founded the Achaemenid Empire in 550 BCE by overthrowing the Median Empire, establishing a model of governance based on religious and cultural toleration.

- The satrapy system - regional provinces governed by appointed satraps - allowed Persia to administer a vast, diverse empire while maintaining central authority.

- Darius I came to power in 522 BCE after suppressing a major dynastic crisis, then spent years crushing rebellions across the empire before consolidating control.

- Darius reorganized the satrapies, standardized taxation, and created royal inspectors to prevent regional officials from accumulating independent power.

- Persian royal roads and courier networks connected the empire physically, enabling rapid communication, military movement, and trade.

- Religious policy was a key instrument of imperial control: Cyrus adopted the gods of conquered peoples to legitimize his rule, while Darius framed Persian kingship as divinely ordained by Ahura Mazda.

- Together, Cyrus and Darius created the first recognizably imperial identity - one that tolerated diversity while insisting on Persian supremacy - a model that influenced empires for centuries to come.

What Cyrus and Darius invented was not merely a state. It was a template - a proof of concept that an empire could be both vast and coherent, both diverse and unified, both tolerant and demanding. The Persian model of governance would be studied, imitated, and adapted by rulers from Alexander the Great to the Roman emperors who came after him. Whether Persia itself could live up to its own invention proved, as later chapters will show, considerably harder.

Part 2
Building the Imperial Machine

Chapter 4:
The King of Kings

The Rock Relief at Naqsh-e Rostam: Divine Investiture of Ardashir I

A god did not sit on the Sasanian throne. But the man who did sat very close to one.

When Ardashir I overthrew the last Parthian king in 224 AD and declared himself ruler of a new Persian empire, he did not simply claim a crown. He claimed the cosmos. His title - *Shahanshah*, King of Kings - was not a boast or a flourish. It was a theological statement, a political architecture, and a warning, all compressed into two words. To understand the Sasanian Empire is, in large part, to understand what those two words meant to the people who lived beneath them, and to the rulers who wielded them for more than four centuries.

From 224 to 651 AD, the Sasanian Empire stood as one of the ancient world's great powers, locked in near-constant rivalry with Rome and later Byzantium to the west, while managing pressure from the Kushans and Hephthalites to the east. Its kings commanded armies, administered vast territories, and presided over a civilization of remarkable cultural depth. But the engine beneath all of it - the force that legitimized conquest, justified hierarchy, and gave the empire its distinctive identity - was the idea of sacred kingship. That idea was older than the Sasanians themselves. They simply perfected it.

What follows is an examination of the institution at the heart of the empire: the king himself. What the title *Shahanshah* actually meant in practice. How divine authority was constructed and communicated. What rituals and symbols sustained royal power. And where, despite all the ceremony and ideology, the limits of that power quietly began.

What "King of Kings" Really Meant

The title *Shahanshah* - King of Kings - sounds, to modern ears, like hyperbole. It was anything but.

Under the Sasanian system, the empire was not a flat hierarchy with one ruler commanding a uniform population. It was a layered world of subordinate kings, regional lords, powerful nobles, and vassal rulers, all of whom owed their authority - at least in theory - to the man at the apex. The "kings" over whom the Shahanshah ruled were real. Some governed entire territories. Some commanded armies. Some held ancient bloodlines that predated the Sasanians entirely. The title acknowledged this complexity while simultaneously subordinating it.

Ardashir I understood this from the moment he founded the empire. His rise between roughly 208 and 224 AD was not a sudden coup but a sustained campaign of conquest and consolidation, dismantling the Parthian Arsacid dynasty piece by piece. When he finally emerged victorious, he inherited a world of competing power centers. His solution was not to eliminate them but to reframe them - to position himself not merely as the strongest king, but as the king whose authority encompassed and legitimized all others.

This was a distinctly Persian inheritance. The Sasanians were acutely conscious of themselves as heirs to the Achaemenid Empire, the great Persian dynasty that had ruled from the sixth to the fourth century BC. Cyrus the Great, Darius, Xerxes - these were not distant legends to the Sasanian court. They were ancestors, models, and sources of legitimacy. By reviving the Achaemenid title and its associated ideology, Ardashir was doing something politically sophisticated: reaching back across centuries to claim a continuity of Persian greatness that the Parthians, in Sasanian eyes, had interrupted.

This revival of Iranian nationalism was one of the empire's defining features. Language, religion, and royal symbolism were all marshaled in service of a Persian identity that set the Sasanians apart from their predecessors. The Parthians had been relatively tolerant of Hellenistic cultural influence - a legacy of Alexander's conquests. The Sasanians deliberately pushed back, emphasizing indigenous Iranian traditions and anchoring their rule in a specifically Persian past.

So when a Sasanian king called himself King of Kings, he was making several claims at once. He was asserting supremacy over all subordinate rulers within the empire. He was positioning himself as the legitimate heir of ancient Persian greatness. And he was declaring, to Rome and Byzantium and every rival power on the horizon, that the Persian empire had not ended. It had returned.

Divine Investiture and Symbolism

Power, in the Sasanian world, did not flow from armies alone. It flowed from God.

The Sasanians were Zoroastrian, adherents of one of the world's oldest monotheistic traditions, centered on the supreme deity Ahura Mazda. In Zoroastrian theology, the cosmic struggle between light and darkness, truth and falsehood, was not merely spiritual. It was political. A righteous king was not just a competent administrator. He was a participant in the divine order, a defender of truth against chaos. His authority was not self-generated. It was bestowed.

This concept had a name: *farr*, or royal glory - a divine radiance that marked the legitimate king as chosen by Ahura Mazda. A king who possessed *farr* was invincible, blessed, cosmically sanctioned. A king who lost it - through wickedness, weakness, or defeat - had been abandoned by heaven itself. The idea gave Sasanian kingship a theological dimension that no army could fully replicate. You could defeat a king in battle. But you could not argue with divine selection.

Rock reliefs carved into cliff faces across the empire made this theology visible in stone. At sites like Naqsh-e Rostam and Naqsh-e Rajab, Ardashir I and his successors commissioned monumental carvings depicting the moment of divine investiture: the king receiving a ring - the symbol of royal authority - directly from Ahura Mazda. In these images, god and king face each other as near-equals, the divine and the earthly in direct communion. The message was unmistakable. This king rules because heaven chose him.

Shapur I, Ardashir's son and the empire's second ruler, continued this tradition while expanding it. His rock reliefs at Naqsh-e Rostam famously depicted his military victories over Rome - including the humiliation of the Roman Emperor Valerian, shown kneeling before the Sasanian king. But even in these martial images, the divine framework was present. Shapur's victories were not merely military achievements. They were evidence of divine favor. Heaven had not just permitted his conquests - it had ordained them.

Symbolism extended to the royal regalia as well. The elaborate crown worn by each Sasanian king was not a generic symbol of rulership. Each monarch had his own distinctive crown, depicted on coins and reliefs, so that the image of the crown itself became a kind of royal signature. Fire - sacred in Zoroastrian tradition - featured prominently in royal iconography. The eternal flame was not decorative. It was a living symbol of the divine presence that sustained the empire.

Royal Rituals and Court Culture

Ideology required performance. The Sasanian court understood this with remarkable sophistication.

Audiences with the king were elaborately choreographed events, designed to communicate the vast distance between the ruler and everyone else. Courtiers approached the throne through layers of ceremony - prostration, formal address, prescribed gestures - each step reinforcing the hierarchical order that placed the Shahanshah at its summit. Foreign ambassadors who entered the Sasanian court were not simply meeting a powerful ruler. They were entering a staged cosmology, in which every detail of dress, movement, and speech had been calibrated to convey a single message: this man is not like other men.

The court itself was a world of extraordinary refinement. Sasanian culture produced remarkable achievements in art, architecture, and music, and the royal court stood at the center of that cultural production. Elaborate feasts, formal hunts, and ceremonial processions were not mere entertainment. They were political theater - opportunities to display royal magnificence, reinforce social hierarchies, and bind the nobility to the crown through shared participation in a culture of splendor.

Music held a particular place in court life. Sasanian court musicians were celebrated figures, and the tradition of Persian court music that would later influence Islamic civilization had deep roots in this period. The legendary musician Barbad, associated with the court of Khosrow II, became so celebrated that stories of his artistry survived for centuries after the empire's fall.

Hunting was another arena of royal performance. The royal hunt - depicted extensively in Sasanian art, particularly on silver plates and bowls - was not simply recreation. It was a demonstration of royal virtue: courage, skill, mastery over the natural world. A king who hunted lions was a king who could conquer chaos. The imagery was deliberate, and it reached audiences far beyond the court through the circulation of luxury objects bearing these scenes.

A fusion of ancient Iranian traditions with a more hierarchical worldview - one that would have been recognizable to contemporaries in Byzantium or Gupta India - gave Sasanian court culture its distinctive character. It was simultaneously archaic and cosmopolitan, drawing on centuries of Persian tradition while absorbing influences from the wider world the empire touched.

Propaganda Through Titles and Imagery

Every coin the Sasanian empire minted was a small piece of propaganda.

On one side: the king's portrait, with his distinctive crown. On the other: a Zoroastrian fire altar, flanked by attendants. In a world without mass media, coins were one of the most efficient ways to circulate an image and a message across a vast territory. Every transaction - every merchant, soldier, and farmer who handled Sasanian silver - encountered the king's face and the sacred flame. The message was quiet but relentless: this is who rules, and this is why.

Titles were equally deliberate. Sasanian royal inscriptions did not simply name the king. They accumulated titles in layers, each one adding another dimension to the royal identity. "King of Kings of Iran and non-Iran," "whose lineage is from the gods," "associate of the gods" - these were not empty formulas. They were carefully constructed claims, each phrase doing specific ideological work. The reference to "Iran and non-Iran" acknowledged the empire's multi-ethnic reality while centering Iranian identity as its core. The divine lineage claims connected the king to Ahura Mazda's cosmic order.

Rock reliefs served a similar function on a monumental scale. Carved at prominent sites along major routes, they were visible to travelers, merchants, and armies moving through the empire. They did not require literacy. A carving of the king receiving the ring of divine authority from Ahura Mazda communicated its message to anyone who looked at it. This was propaganda in the most literal sense - the propagation of a specific image of power, repeated across media and across centuries.

The Sasanians also used their rivalry with Rome and Byzantium as a source of prestige. Shapur I's depiction of the captured Roman Emperor Valerian was not just a military trophy. It was a theological statement: the King of Kings had humbled the ruler of the western world. Heaven had spoken. The image was carved in stone and meant to last forever.

The Limits of Absolute Power

For all its theological architecture, Sasanian kingship was not truly absolute.

The empire's nobility - the great aristocratic families who controlled vast estates and commanded private armies - were never fully subordinated to the crown. They were essential partners in the imperial project, providing military manpower, administrative capacity, and regional control that the king could not supply alone.

This made them indispensable. Indispensable partners are rarely powerless ones.

The Zoroastrian priesthood, the Magi, represented another check. As guardians of religious orthodoxy and administrators of the fire temples that dotted the empire, they wielded enormous social authority. A king who alienated the priesthood risked losing the religious legitimacy that underpinned his entire claim to rule. The *farr* could, in theory, be withdrawn - and the priests were its interpreters.

The reign of Khosrow II, known as Khosrow Parviz, illustrated these tensions with painful clarity. His rule began with military success - at one point, Sasanian armies pushed deep into Byzantine territory, capturing Jerusalem and Egypt - but ended in catastrophe. Internal strife, noble rebellion, and the exhaustion of prolonged warfare against Byzantium left the empire structurally weakened. Khosrow II was eventually overthrown and killed by his own nobles in 628 AD, a stark reminder that the divine right of kings had earthly limits.

Within two decades of his death, the Arab conquests had swept through the empire entirely. Yazdgerd III, the last Sasanian king, died in 651 AD - not in battle, but murdered by a local miller while fleeing his pursuers. The King of Kings, the associate of the gods, ended his days as a fugitive.

The fall was swift, but the idea endured. The imagery, the titles, the concept of sacred Persian kingship - all of it passed into the cultural inheritance of the Islamic world that followed, shaping how rulers in the region would present themselves for centuries to come.

Quick Summary

- The title *Shahanshah* - King of Kings - was a theological and political claim, not merely an honorific, asserting supremacy over all subordinate rulers within the empire.

- Ardashir I founded the Sasanian Empire in 224 AD by overthrowing the Parthians, deliberately positioning himself as heir to the ancient Achaemenid Persian tradition.

- Divine legitimacy rested on the concept of *farr* - a God-given royal glory bestowed by Ahura Mazda - making the king's authority sacred, not merely political.

- Rock reliefs, coins, and royal inscriptions served as sophisticated propaganda tools, communicating the king's divine mandate across a vast, multilingual empire.

- Court culture was elaborately ceremonial, using ritual, art, music, and the royal hunt to reinforce hierarchy and project royal magnificence.

- Despite its ideology of absolute divine rule, Sasanian kingship was constrained in practice by powerful noble families and the Zoroastrian priesthood.

- The empire's decline accelerated through internal strife - exemplified by the fall of Khosrow II in 628 AD - before the Arab conquests ended Sasanian rule entirely by 651 AD.

- The concept of sacred Persian kingship outlasted the empire itself, flowing into the political culture of the Islamic world that inherited its territories.

The last Sasanian king died as a fugitive, but the idea he embodied refused to disappear. Empires end; the myths that sustained them have a habit of surviving. What the Sasanians had built - this intricate fusion of divine right, Persian identity, and royal spectacle - would be borrowed, adapted, and reimagined by every power that rose in their wake. The King of Kings was gone. But the idea of what a king should be lingered on, waiting for new hands to claim it.

Chapter 5:
The Machinery of Empire

An empire is not built on conquest alone. Armies can seize territory in a season, but holding it - taxing it, administering it, keeping its roads passable and its grain flowing - requires something far less glamorous and far more durable: paperwork.

Behind every Roman emperor stood a vast, intricate system of governance that made the empire function from one day to the next. It was a machine built from habit, hierarchy, and hard-won administrative logic. Without it, the legions would have had nothing to defend. Without it, Rome would have been not an empire but a very large raid.

The story of that machine - how it was built, how it operated, and how it shaped the lives of millions of people who never set foot in the capital - is, in many ways, the story of how power actually works. From the reorganization of government under Augustus to the elaborations introduced by Claudius, from the tax collectors of distant provinces to the record-keepers who tracked it all, Roman administration reveals the empire's true foundation: not marble, but method.

Structure of the Imperial Bureaucracy

When Augustus became Rome's first emperor in the decades following Julius Caesar's assassination, he inherited a republic whose institutions were designed for a city-state, not a Mediterranean superpower. The Senate still existed. The old magistracies still carried their titles. But the reality of power had shifted irrevocably, and Augustus was shrewd enough to understand that the machinery of governance needed to shift with it.

What Augustus built was not a bureaucracy in the modern sense - no vast ministry buildings, no standardized forms in triplicate. He created a framework: a set of relationships, responsibilities, and chains of command that gave the emperor real control over the empire's resources and personnel. He reorganized the Roman government so that key functions - military command, provincial oversight, financial management - flowed upward toward the emperor rather than outward toward the Senate.

This was a quiet revolution. Augustus kept the old republican forms intact while hollowing them out, replacing their substance with a new imperial logic. Senators still debated. Consuls still held their ancient offices. But the real decisions - who governed which province, how the legions were funded, where the grain supply was directed - were increasingly made by men who answered to the emperor alone.

The system Augustus established was elaborated and sharpened by his successors, but it was the fourth emperor, Claudius, who transformed it most decisively. Claudius, who ruled from 41 to 54 CE, had a reputation among his contemporaries as an unlikely emperor - bookish, physically awkward, underestimated by almost everyone around him. That underestimation turned out to be Rome's good fortune.

Claudius brought to the throne an administrator's mind. He expanded the imperial bureaucracy substantially, creating new departments staffed by freedmen - former slaves who owed their status and their loyalty directly to the emperor. These men handled correspondence, finances, legal petitions, and administrative records. They were not senators or aristocrats. They were professionals, and their professionalism made the empire run.

The effect was a bureaucracy that could manage complexity at scale. Where Augustus had built the skeleton, Claudius added the muscle. By the height of the early empire, Rome possessed an administrative apparatus capable of coordinating governance across territories stretching from Britain to Mesopotamia - a feat that would have been unthinkable under the old republic.

Provincial Governance

Rome's empire was not a single, uniform territory. It was a patchwork of regions, cultures, languages, and local traditions, stitched together under Roman authority but never fully homogenized. Governing this patchwork required a system flexible enough to accommodate local variation while firm enough to extract taxes, maintain order, and project Roman power.

Provinces were the basic unit of that system. Each province was administered by a governor - either a senator appointed by the Senate or an imperial legate appointed directly by the emperor, depending on the province's strategic importance and stability. Frontier provinces with active legions tended to fall under imperial control; quieter, more settled provinces might remain under senatorial oversight.

A governor's role was broad and demanding. He commanded whatever military forces were stationed in his province, presided over the highest courts, oversaw the collection of taxes, and managed relations with local elites. He was, in effect, a miniature emperor within his territory - powerful, largely autonomous in day-to-day decisions, but ultimately accountable to Rome.

That accountability was enforced imperfectly. Communication across the empire was slow, measured in weeks or months rather than hours. A governor in Syria or Britain operated with considerable independence simply because the logistics of oversight made close supervision impossible. This created opportunities for both exceptional competence and spectacular corruption.

Claudius's reforms helped address some of these vulnerabilities. By strengthening the administrative infrastructure at the center - improving record-keeping, clarifying chains of command, professionalizing key functions - he made it harder for provincial governors to operate entirely without scrutiny. Better administration at the center meant more consistent governance at the periphery, and the populations of outlying regions felt the difference in the quality of roads, courts, and public services.

Provincial governance was never perfect. But at its best, it represented a genuine achievement: a system capable of delivering something resembling order and justice across an enormous and diverse territory.

Taxation Systems

If the bureaucracy was the empire's nervous system, taxation was its blood supply. Rome's military, its infrastructure, its grain distributions, its public buildings - all of it depended on a steady flow of revenue extracted from the provinces and funneled back to the center.

Roman taxation took several forms. The most significant was the *tributum*, a direct tax levied on land and persons in the provinces. Rates and methods varied by region, reflecting the patchwork nature of provincial administration, but the underlying logic was consistent: conquered peoples paid for the privilege of Roman governance.

Indirect taxes added further layers. Customs duties were levied on goods moving through ports and across provincial boundaries. Inheritance taxes applied to Roman citizens. Fees attached to the manumission of slaves. Taken together, these revenues constituted a fiscal system of considerable sophistication - not always fair, not always efficiently collected, but capable of sustaining one of the largest military and administrative establishments the ancient world had ever seen.

Tax collection itself was a complicated business. In the early empire, Rome relied heavily on tax farmers - private contractors who paid the state a lump sum upfront in exchange for the right to collect taxes in a given region, keeping whatever they could extract above that sum. The system was efficient from Rome's perspective but notoriously brutal in practice. Tax farmers had every incentive to squeeze as much as possible from local populations, and they frequently did.

Over time, the imperial government moved toward more direct collection methods, bringing tax administration increasingly under official control. This shift was part of the broader professionalization of the bureaucracy - a recognition that the empire's long-term stability depended on extracting revenue in ways that didn't permanently alienate the populations being taxed.

The tension between fiscal necessity and local tolerance was never fully resolved. But the fact that Rome managed to sustain its tax system across centuries and continents speaks to the underlying durability of the administrative machinery that supported it.

Record-Keeping and Control

An empire that cannot count what it owns cannot govern what it rules. Rome understood this. Across the empire, officials maintained records of land ownership, population counts, tax assessments, military rosters, legal decisions, and administrative correspondence. This documentary infrastructure was the connective tissue of imperial governance.

Censuses were conducted periodically to assess the taxable population and resources of the provinces. Land surveys established the basis for property taxes. Military records tracked the strength and disposition of the legions. Legal archives preserved the decisions of courts and governors, creating a body of precedent that gave Roman law its remarkable consistency across geography and time.

Much of this record-keeping was carried out by the same class of imperial freedmen that Claudius had elevated to prominence. These men - skilled in literacy, numeracy, and administrative procedure -

formed a kind of permanent civil service that persisted across changes of emperor and shifts in political fortune. While emperors came and went, often violently, the clerks and secretaries who maintained the records kept the machinery running.

This continuity was one of the empire's great strengths. Administrative knowledge was not lost when a governor died or an emperor was overthrown. The state had a memory - an institutional capacity to track obligations, enforce agreements, and maintain consistency over time.

Control, in this sense, was not primarily about coercion. It was about information. The emperor who knew how much grain his provinces produced, how many soldiers he could field, and how much revenue he could expect was an emperor who could plan, respond, and govern. Record-keeping was power made legible.

The Role of the Nobility

For all the professionalization that Claudius introduced, the Roman nobility remained central to how the empire actually functioned. Senators, equestrians, and local aristocrats across the provinces were not merely decorative. They were the human infrastructure through which Roman authority was exercised and Roman culture was transmitted.

At the top of this hierarchy sat the senatorial class - the old aristocracy of Rome, whose members filled the most prestigious governorships, commanded the most important legions, and occupied the highest offices of the state. Their cooperation was essential. An emperor who alienated the Senate entirely risked not just political opposition but administrative paralysis, since senators provided much of the personnel through which the empire was governed.

Below the senators stood the equestrians - a broader class of wealthy Romans who filled a wide range of administrative and military roles.

As the imperial bureaucracy expanded, equestrians became increasingly important, taking on positions that had once been reserved for senators or that were newly created to meet the demands of a growing administrative apparatus. Claudius's use of imperial freedmen for key secretarial roles was controversial precisely because it seemed to bypass the equestrian class that might otherwise have expected such appointments.

Beyond Rome itself, local elites in the provinces played an indispensable role. Roman governance worked in large part because it co-opted existing power structures rather than replacing them entirely. Local aristocrats served as intermediaries between the Roman administration and the local population - collecting taxes, maintaining order, and lending the Roman system a degree of local legitimacy it could not have manufactured on its own.

This arrangement had a certain elegance. Rome got reliable local partners who understood their communities. Local elites got Roman backing for their authority, access to Roman legal protections, and the prestige of association with the empire's power. Both sides had reasons to make the relationship work.

Early in the fourth century, significant changes to the structure of the imperial state began to reshape the distribution of political power within this system. The precise nature of those changes, and their long-term consequences, would ripple through the empire's remaining centuries - a reminder that even the most durable machinery requires constant adjustment to keep running.

Key Takeaways

- Augustus reorganized Roman government to centralize power in the emperor's hands while preserving the outward forms of the republic.

- Claudius significantly expanded the imperial bureaucracy, staffing key positions with professional freedmen who owed their loyalty directly to the emperor.

- Provincial governors held broad military, judicial, and financial authority within their territories, but slow communications and vast distances made oversight uneven.

- Roman taxation drew on both direct taxes (the *tributum* on land and persons) and indirect taxes (customs, inheritance, manumission fees), sustaining the empire's military and infrastructure.

- Tax collection evolved from private tax farmers toward more direct official control, reflecting the broader professionalization of imperial administration.

- Systematic record-keeping - censuses, land surveys, military rosters, legal archives - gave the state an institutional memory that outlasted individual emperors.

- Local elites across the provinces served as essential intermediaries, translating imperial authority into local reality in exchange for Roman backing and prestige.

- Fourth-century reforms to the imperial structure had lasting effects on the distribution of political power within the empire.

Empires are remembered for their battles and their emperors, their monuments and their myths. But what made Rome endure for centuries was something quieter: the patient accumulation of administrative habit, the slow construction of systems capable of governing millions of people across an enormous and varied world. Augustus imagined it. Claudius built it. Countless anonymous clerks, tax collectors, and local officials kept it running, day after day, decade after decade. That, in the end, is what an empire actually is - not a throne, but the machinery behind it. What happened when that machinery began to strain under new pressures is a question the chapters ahead will answer.

Chapter 6:
Law, Order, and the Governed Empire

To rule millions of people scattered across a territory stretching from Mesopotamia to Central Asia, the Sasanian kings needed more than cavalry and fortified walls. They needed something subtler, more pervasive, and ultimately more durable: a system of rules that could reach into every village, every market transaction, every inheritance dispute, and every question of who owed what to whom. Armies could conquer. Only law could govern.

Why Law Mattered in the Sasanian World

Between 224 and 651 CE, the Sasanian Empire rose from a regional Persian kingdom to one of the ancient world's great powers - a rival to Rome and Byzantium in the west, a counterweight to the Kushans and later the Turks in the east. At its height, it encompassed dozens of languages, ethnicities, and religious communities. Holding all of that together required administration on a scale that few empires before it had attempted.

Law was the architecture of that administration. It defined who owned land and who worked it, who could testify in court and who could not, what a widow was owed after her husband's death, and what a merchant could expect when a contract was broken. It told judges how to weigh evidence, told priests how to handle sacred property, and told provincial governors how far their authority extended before it bumped against someone else's.

What makes the Sasanian legal tradition particularly fascinating is that it was never purely secular. Religious and legal authority were deeply intertwined from the beginning, and the empire's official faith - Zoroastrianism - shaped not just the rituals of daily life but the very foundations of how justice was conceived and administered. To understand Sasanian law is to understand how a civilization tried to make the divine will legible in everyday human affairs.

Legal Traditions and Sources

Any legal system is only as strong as the texts and traditions that underpin it. For the Sasanians, those foundations were ancient, layered, and explicitly sacred.

Zoroastrianism provided the empire's ideological core, and its scriptures - the Avesta - served as far more than religious literature. They were legal documents. The Avesta contained detailed provisions governing property, contracts, family relations, and ritual obligations, and Zoroastrian priests, known as *mobads*, were trained not only as religious officiants but as legal interpreters. When a dispute arose over an inheritance or a marriage contract, the priest who adjudicated it was drawing on the same textual tradition that governed fire temple rituals and cosmological prayers.

This integration of religious and legal authority was not incidental - it was structural. The Sasanian state was explicitly a Zoroastrian empire, and its kings derived legitimacy in part from their role as protectors and enforcers of the divine order. Law, in this framework, was not merely a human convenience. It was an expression of *asha* - the Zoroastrian concept of truth, righteousness, and cosmic order. To break the law was not just a civil offense. It was a transgression against the fabric of the universe.

Alongside the Avestan tradition, the Sasanians also inherited and adapted older Mesopotamian legal customs. The empire's heartland in what is now Iraq and Iran had been home to sophisticated legal cultures for millennia, and Sasanian administrators were pragmatic enough to incorporate local practices where they served imperial purposes. The result was a legal system simultaneously rooted in ancient Persian religious tradition and flexible enough to function across diverse populations.

Perhaps the most remarkable surviving evidence of Sasanian legal practice is the *Mātakdān ī Hazār Dādestān* - the "Book of a Thousand Judgments." Compiled in the late Sasanian period, this collection of legal opinions and case decisions offers a rare window into how the law actually operated in practice. It covers everything from property disputes and guardianship to the rights of religious minorities and the obligations of debtors. Reading it, one gets a sense not of abstract legal philosophy but of a living, working system grappling with the messy realities of human life.

Law as a Tool of Imperial Administration

A legal system can be a philosophical achievement and still fail as an administrative tool. The Sasanians understood this. Their legal apparatus was designed not just to resolve disputes but to organize the empire - to make it legible, manageable, and extractable.

Taxation was perhaps the most immediate expression of this imperative. The empire's revenues depended on knowing who owned what, which meant that property law and land registration were not abstract concerns but urgent fiscal necessities. Sasanian administrators maintained records of landholding, assessed agricultural yields, and used legal mechanisms to ensure that obligations to the crown were met. The law, in this sense, was the empire's accounting system as much as its moral framework.

Contract law served a similar function. Long-distance trade connected the Sasanian Empire to India, China, the Byzantine world, and the Arabian Peninsula, and merchants needed enforceable agreements to operate across those distances. Sasanian law provided mechanisms for written contracts, witnessed transactions, and legal recourse when agreements were broken. The empire's position at the center of Eurasian trade routes made reliable commercial law not just useful but economically essential.

Family law was another domain where legal administration intersected with imperial governance. Marriage, inheritance, and guardianship were not purely private matters - they determined how property passed between generations, how noble families maintained their wealth and status, and how the empire's social hierarchy reproduced itself over time. Sasanian law governing these areas was detailed and often surprisingly sophisticated, with provisions for different categories of marriage, the rights of children from various unions, and the obligations of guardians toward their wards.

The legal system also served as a mechanism of religious administration. Zoroastrian institutions - fire temples, priestly colleges, religious endowments - held significant property and required legal frameworks to manage it. The *mobads* who ran these institutions were simultaneously religious authorities and legal actors, and the law gave them tools to protect sacred property, enforce religious obligations, and adjudicate disputes within the Zoroastrian community.

What emerges from all of this is a picture of law not as a separate sphere of life but as the connective tissue of the entire imperial project. It linked the king's authority to the village judge, the priest's religious role to the administrator's fiscal one, and the ancient sacred texts to the practical demands of governing a complex, multiethnic empire.

Social Order and Hierarchy

Sasanian society was explicitly hierarchical, and the law both reflected and enforced that hierarchy. The empire organized its population into broad estates - roughly, the priests, the warriors, the scribes and administrators, and the farmers and artisans - and legal status tracked closely with social position.

Priests occupied the apex of this system, at least in theory. As interpreters of divine law and custodians of the sacred fire temples, the *mobads* held authority that no secular official could easily override. Their testimony carried particular weight in legal proceedings, and their institutions enjoyed protections and privileges that other social groups did not.

Warriors - the nobility and military aristocracy - formed the second estate, and their legal standing reflected their social power. Noble families controlled vast landholdings, commanded private retinues, and exercised significant local authority. The law recognized their elevated status in matters of testimony, compensation for injury, and the rights of their dependents.

Below them, the scribes and administrators formed a literate middle class whose legal identity was tied to their service to the state. And at the base of the hierarchy, farmers and artisans - the vast majority of the population - enjoyed legal protections but operated within a framework that consistently prioritized the interests of those above them.

This stratification was not merely descriptive. It was prescriptive. The law assigned different values to the lives and testimony of people from different estates, and penalties for crimes often varied depending on the social status of both victim and perpetrator. Injuring a nobleman carried different legal consequences than injuring a farmer, and the testimony of a priest weighed more heavily than that of a craftsman.

Religious minorities occupied a complicated position within this framework. Zoroastrianism was the state religion, and non-Zoroastrians - Christians, Jews, Buddhists, Manichaeans, and others - lived under a legal regime that formally subordinated them to the Zoroastrian majority. In practice, however, the empire was often pragmatic about religious diversity. Minority communities maintained their own internal legal systems for matters of personal status and religious practice, and Sasanian rulers periodically extended protections to minority groups when it served political or economic purposes. The relationship between the Zoroastrian legal mainstream and the empire's many religious minorities was never simple, and it shifted considerably across the four centuries of Sasanian rule.

Enforcement, Authority, and Local Power

Writing laws is one thing. Enforcing them across a territory the size of the Sasanian Empire is something else entirely.

Judicial authority in the Sasanian system was distributed across several overlapping institutions. At the local level, priests and village elders handled most everyday disputes - the kind of quarrels over water rights, livestock, and inheritance that made up the bulk of legal business in any agrarian society. These local authorities operated within the framework of Zoroastrian legal tradition, but they also drew on customary practices that varied from region to region.

At higher levels, the empire maintained a more formal judicial apparatus. Provincial governors exercised legal authority within their territories, and the king himself stood at the apex of the system as the ultimate source of justice. Royal justice was not merely symbolic - Sasanian kings are recorded as intervening in legal disputes, issuing rulings, and occasionally overriding lower-level decisions. The image of the just king as the guarantor of order was central to Sasanian royal ideology, and it had practical as well as symbolic dimensions.

The *mobads* played a dual role throughout this system. As religious authorities, they interpreted sacred law. As legal officials, they presided over courts, authenticated documents, and served as witnesses in major transactions. This dual function gave the priestly class enormous practical power, since controlling the interpretation of law meant controlling the outcomes of disputes.

Local power was a persistent complicating factor. The Sasanian Empire was not a modern centralized state with a professional bureaucracy reaching into every corner of its territory. Noble families, local chieftains, and religious institutions all exercised real authority in their domains, and the relationship between central imperial law and local custom was often one of negotiation rather than simple command. The empire's legal system had to be flexible enough to accommodate this reality while still maintaining enough coherence to function as a genuinely imperial institution.

Justice in Practice: Between Ideal and Reality

Every legal system contains a gap between its stated ideals and its actual operation. The Sasanian system was no exception.

The *Mātakdān ī Hazār Dādestān* and other surviving legal texts present a picture of careful, principled adjudication - judges weighing evidence, consulting precedents, applying religious principles to specific cases. There is no reason to doubt that this ideal was sometimes achieved. The sophistication of the surviving legal literature suggests a tradition of serious legal scholarship and genuine commitment to principled decision-making.

But the same sources also reveal the pressures that bent those ideals. Social hierarchy meant that the powerful had structural advantages in legal proceedings. Access to learned priests who could master complex legal arguments was not equally distributed. Local strongmen could influence outcomes in ways that no written law could fully prevent. And in a system where religious and legal authority overlapped so completely, the line between enforcing divine order and enforcing the interests of the priestly class was not always easy to draw.

Historians differ on how to weigh these tensions. Some emphasize the genuine achievements of Sasanian legal culture - its sophistication, its longevity, and its influence on later Islamic legal traditions that absorbed and transformed many of its elements after the Arab conquests of the seventh century. Others point to the ways the system entrenched inequality and limited the legal standing of women, non-Zoroastrians, and lower social orders.

Both assessments are probably right. The Sasanian legal system was a genuine intellectual and administrative achievement, and it was also a system designed by elites to serve the interests of a hierarchical society. These two things are not contradictory. They describe most legal systems in most times and places.

Key Takeaways

- The Sasanian Empire (224-651 CE) developed a sophisticated legal system that blended Zoroastrian religious principles with practical administrative needs.

- The Avesta, Zoroastrianism's sacred scriptures, served as a foundational legal text, and Zoroastrian priests (*mobads*) functioned simultaneously as religious and legal authorities.

- Law served as a critical tool of imperial administration, governing taxation, land ownership, commercial contracts, and family relations across a vast and diverse empire.

- Sasanian society was organized into formal estates - priests, warriors, administrators, and farmers - and legal status tracked closely with social position, with different rights and protections assigned to different groups.

- Religious minorities maintained internal legal autonomy for personal and religious matters, though they operated within a framework that formally privileged the Zoroastrian majority.

- Judicial authority was distributed across local priests, provincial governors, and the king himself, with the Zoroastrian priestly class holding particular influence as interpreters of sacred law.

- The *Mātakdān ī Hazār Dādestān* (Book of a Thousand Judgments) survives as a rare window into how Sasanian law actually operated in practice.

- Sasanian legal traditions influenced later Islamic legal culture after the Arab conquests, giving this system a legacy that extended well beyond the empire's own lifespan.

What the Sasanians built was not just a legal code but a vision of how divine order could be made to function on earth - imperfectly, unevenly, and with all the compromises that real governance demands, but with genuine ambition and considerable sophistication.

When Arab armies swept across the empire in the seventh century, they did not erase that tradition. They inherited it, argued with it, and ultimately transformed it into something new. The law outlasted the empire that created it.

Part 3
Religion, Society, and Power

Chapter 7:
Fire and Faith - Zoroastrianism as State Power

The Geography of Sacred Fire: Zoroastrian Fire Temples Across the Empire

When Ardashir I overthrew the last Parthian king in 224 AD and declared himself ruler of a new Persian empire, he did not simply seize a throne. He seized a cosmos. From the very first years of

Sasanian rule, the sacred fire burning at the heart of every Zoroastrian temple was not merely a religious symbol - it was a political statement, a declaration that the king ruled not by force alone, but by divine right, with the god Ohrmazd himself as the ultimate guarantor of imperial order.

That fusion of faith and power would define the Sasanian Empire for more than four centuries. In the Sasanian world, religion was not separate from the state. It *was* the state. The priesthood held institutional power rivaling the court. Fire temples operated as both spiritual centers and economic engines. The king's right to rule rested not on bloodline alone but on a theological claim - that Ohrmazd had chosen him to defend creation itself. To grasp how the Sasanian Empire functioned, you have to understand its religion - not as a backdrop to politics, but as the operating system that made politics possible.

A World Divided Between Light and Darkness

Zoroastrianism is one of the world's oldest monotheistic religions, built around the teachings of the prophet Zarathustra. At its center stands a cosmic struggle between two opposing forces: Ohrmazd, the supreme god of light, truth, and creation, and Ahriman, the destructive spirit of darkness and chaos. Every human being, in this worldview, is a participant in that struggle. Every choice, every action, every word carries moral weight. The universe itself is a battlefield, and humanity is not a passive audience - it is the army.

This dualistic framework gave Zoroastrianism an unusual moral urgency. Life was not something to be endured or transcended; it was something to be fought for. The good creation - the physical world of light, fire, water, earth, and living things - was sacred and worth defending. Ritual purity mattered enormously, because pollution of the sacred elements was understood as a victory for Ahriman.

Fire occupied a special place in this theology. It was not worshipped as a god in itself, but venerated as the most visible symbol of Ohrmazd's divine light - a living presence of truth and purity in a world constantly threatened by darkness. To tend a sacred fire was to participate in the cosmic order. To let it die was an act of profound spiritual failure.

Three grades of sacred fire existed in the Zoroastrian tradition, each with its own ritual significance and social meaning. The highest grade, the Bahram fire, required the most elaborate consecration and represented the highest concentration of divine presence. These fires were not merely ceremonial. They were understood as living entities, requiring constant attention, feeding, and protection.

Alongside fire, the religion placed enormous emphasis on truth - *asha* in the Avestan language, the sacred tongue of Zoroastrian scripture. Asha encompassed not just honesty but cosmic order itself: the right relationship between all things, the proper functioning of the universe. Its opposite, *druj*, meant the lie - but also disorder, corruption, and the forces that sought to unravel creation.

For a new empire looking to legitimize its rule and unify a vast, diverse population, this theology was extraordinarily useful. A king who stood for asha, who defended the sacred fires and upheld divine order, was not just a political leader. He was a cosmic warrior.

The Men Who Built the Church

Ardashir I may have founded the Sasanian Empire, but he did not build its religious architecture alone. Two figures in particular shaped the institutional form that Zoroastrianism took under early Sasanian rule: Tansar and Kartēr.

Tansar served Ardashir I in the critical early decades of the empire, working to consolidate Zoroastrian doctrine and establish the authority of the priestly class. His role was partly theological -

organizing and standardizing religious texts and practice - and partly political, helping to define the relationship between the king and the priesthood. He is associated with efforts to bring regional religious variations under a single, centralized orthodoxy. In a newly unified empire that had absorbed many different local traditions, this was no small task.

Kartēr, however, became the most visible and influential religious figure of the early Sasanian period. His career stretched across the reigns of multiple kings, and he rose to a position of extraordinary power within the priestly hierarchy. Under the king Shāpūr I, he served as *ehrpat* - a senior priestly title - and continued accumulating influence long after Shāpūr's death.

What makes Kartēr remarkable is not just his longevity but his self-promotion. He commissioned rock inscriptions - a form of public monument usually reserved for kings - in which he described his own religious achievements in grandiose terms. He boasted of establishing fire temples, of spreading Zoroastrian practice across the empire, and of suppressing rival religions. These inscriptions are among the most direct surviving evidence of how the Sasanian religious establishment understood its own mission.

Kartēr's rise tells us something important about the Sasanian system: the priesthood was not simply subordinate to the king. It was a parallel power structure, with its own hierarchy, its own resources, and its own ambitions. The relationship between king and priest was one of mutual reinforcement - but also, at times, of tension and negotiation.

The priestly class, known as the *magi* or *mowbeds*, controlled access to ritual knowledge, performed the ceremonies that legitimized royal authority, and managed the fire temples that served as the empire's religious infrastructure. Their power was real and institutional. A king who lost the support of the senior priesthood faced serious problems. A priesthood that lost royal patronage faced equally serious ones.

The Sacred Fires That Held an Empire Together

No institution embodied the fusion of religion and state power more completely than the fire temple. Across the Sasanian Empire, fire temples served simultaneously as houses of worship, centers of community life, and visible markers of imperial authority.

Among all the sacred fires of the empire, one stood above the rest: Ādur Gušnasp, located in what is now northwestern Iran. This was the royal fire, the fire of warriors and kings, and it held a special place in Sasanian imperial ritual. New kings were expected to make a pilgrimage to Ādur Gušnasp upon their accession - a journey that could take weeks and that served as a public demonstration of the king's piety and his relationship with the divine order. To skip this pilgrimage was to risk appearing illegitimate in the eyes of both the priesthood and the people.

Two other great fires completed the sacred triad: Ādur Farnbag, associated with the priestly class, and Ādur Burzēn-Mihr, associated with farmers and common people. Together, these three fires symbolized the three-part social order that Zoroastrian ideology projected onto the empire - priests, warriors, and producers - each with their own divine patron flame.

This was not accidental symbolism. It was a carefully constructed religious architecture designed to make the social hierarchy feel cosmically ordained. The king stood at the apex of the warrior class, under the protection of Ādur Gušnasp. The mowbeds tended Ādur Farnbag. Ordinary subjects found their place in the divine order through Ādur Burzēn-Mihr. Every person in the empire, in theory, had a sacred fire that represented their station and their relationship to Ohrmazd.

Fire temples were also economic institutions. They received donations, managed land, and employed staff. The wealth that flowed through them gave the priesthood financial independence and political leverage. A major fire temple was, in effect, a religious corporation - spiritually authoritative, economically powerful, and deeply embedded in local community life.

The King Who Rules by Divine Favor

For the Sasanian kings, Zoroastrianism was not simply a personal faith. It was the ideological foundation of their right to rule.

The concept of *xwarrah* - divine glory or royal fortune - was central to this legitimacy. A king possessed *xwarrah* because Ohrmazd had granted it to him, marking him as the chosen defender of the good creation. This divine favor was not permanent or unconditional; a king who acted unjustly, who failed to uphold asha, could lose it. But as long as he maintained his piety and his proper relationship with the sacred order, his authority was, in a very real theological sense, unquestionable.

Ardashir I understood this from the beginning. By adopting Zoroastrianism as the state religion and positioning himself as the champion of Ohrmazd against the forces of darkness, he transformed a military conquest into a sacred mission. His victory over the Parthians was not merely a political event - it was presented as a cosmic realignment, the restoration of proper order after a period of confusion and decline.

This framing had practical consequences. Opposition to the king was not just treason - it was, in a sense, opposition to the divine order itself. The king's wars could be understood as holy wars, fought in defense of the good creation. And the king's relationship with the priesthood was not optional. He needed their ritual services to maintain his *xwarrah*, and they needed his protection and patronage to maintain their institutions.

The result was a system of mutual dependence that proved, for most of the Sasanian period, remarkably stable. Religion gave the king legitimacy. The king gave religion power. Each reinforced the other in a cycle that endured for centuries.

Orthodoxy, Heresy, and the Limits of Tolerance

That stability had a sharp edge. A state religion is, by definition, a religion with the power to define what is acceptable - and what is not.

The clearest demonstration came during the reign of Bahrām I in the 270s AD, when the Sasanian state turned decisively against Manichaeism. Mani, the founder of this new religious movement, had actually enjoyed a degree of royal tolerance under Shāpūr I, who found his syncretic teachings - blending elements of Zoroastrianism, Christianity, and Buddhism - intellectually interesting. Mani traveled widely, preached openly, and built a substantial following.

But Kartēr, who had spent decades building the institutional power of the Zoroastrian priesthood, saw Manichaeism as a direct threat. Here was a religion that claimed to supersede Zoroastrianism, that drew converts from within the empire, and that operated outside the priestly hierarchy's control. When Bahrām I came to power, Kartēr's influence proved decisive. Mani was arrested, imprisoned, and died in custody around 276 AD. His followers faced persecution across the empire.

The suppression of Manichaeism was not simply religious intolerance. It was a political act, designed to protect the monopoly of the Zoroastrian establishment and to demonstrate that the Sasanian state would not permit rival religious organizations to operate freely within its borders. Other groups - Christians, Jews, Buddhists - occupied complicated and shifting positions within the empire, sometimes tolerated, sometimes persecuted, depending on political circumstances and the attitudes of individual kings.

What the Sasanian system could not easily accommodate was a rival that claimed universal truth and sought active converts. That was the

Zoroastrian priesthood's territory, and Kartēr and his successors defended it aggressively.

Key Figures at a Glance

- **Ardashir I** - Founder of the Sasanian Empire in 224 AD. Established Zoroastrianism as the state religion and framed his rule as divinely sanctioned by Ohrmazd.

- **Tansar** - Senior priest under Ardashir I. Worked to standardize Zoroastrian doctrine and consolidate priestly authority in the early empire.

- **Kartēr** - The most powerful religious figure of the early Sasanian period. Served under multiple kings, commissioned his own rock inscriptions, and played a decisive role in the suppression of Manichaeism.

- **Shāpūr I** - King under whom Kartēr served as *ehrpat*. Initially tolerant of Mani and Manichaeism.

- **Bahrām I** - Reigned 273-276 AD. Backed Kartēr's campaign against Manichaeism; oversaw Mani's imprisonment and death.

- **Mani** - Founder of Manichaeism. Initially tolerated under Shāpūr I, later persecuted and imprisoned under Bahrām I; died in custody around 276 AD.

Quick Summary

- Zoroastrianism centers on a cosmic struggle between Ohrmazd (light, truth, order) and Ahriman (darkness, chaos), with fire serving as the most sacred symbol of divine presence.

- Ardashir I founded the Sasanian Empire in 224 AD and immediately adopted Zoroastrianism as the state religion, framing his rule as divinely sanctioned.

- The concept of *xwarrah* - divine royal glory granted by Ohrmazd - gave Sasanian kings a theological basis for their authority that went beyond military power.

- Two key priestly figures, Tansar and Kartēr, built the institutional infrastructure of Sasanian Zoroastrianism, standardizing doctrine and expanding the fire temple network.

- Fire temples, especially the royal fire Ādur Gušnasp, served as centers of both spiritual life and imperial legitimacy, with new kings making pilgrimage upon accession.

- The three great fires - Ādur Gušnasp, Ādur Farnbag, and Ādur Burzēn-Mihr - symbolized the empire's three-part social order, making hierarchy feel cosmically ordained.

- Under Bahrām I, the Sasanian state suppressed Manichaeism, imprisoning Mani and persecuting his followers, demonstrating that state religion meant state control over spiritual life.

- Religion and political power in the Sasanian Empire were not separate systems that occasionally intersected. They formed a single, integrated structure, each dependent on the other for survival.

What the Sasanian experiment demonstrated, above all, was how completely a state could embed itself in the sacred - and how completely the sacred could embed itself in the state. Priests tended the fires, but kings funded them, armies protected them, and everyone who saw them understood them as proof that the empire stood under divine protection. When that empire eventually fell to the armies of Islam in the seventh century, it was not just a political order that collapsed. An entire sacred world went with it - one that had taken four centuries to build, and whose echoes would shape Persian culture, identity, and religious imagination for centuries beyond.

Chapter 8:
A World of Many Faiths

When the Sasanian king Shapur II launched his persecution of Christians in the fourth century, he did not do so because he found their theology offensive. He did it because they refused to pay double taxes - and because the Roman emperor Constantine had recently converted to Christianity, making every Christian in Persia look, at least from the throne, like a potential enemy agent.

That distinction matters enormously. It tells us something fundamental about how the Sasanian Empire actually worked: not as a monolithic Zoroastrian state crushing all rivals beneath its heel, but as a complex, often pragmatic political organism that used religion as a tool of governance rather than a crusade. The empire that ruled from 224 to 651 CE was home to Zoroastrians, Christians, Jews, Manichaeans, Buddhists, and dozens of smaller communities. Its official faith was Zoroastrianism, its priestly class the Magi, and its sacred fire temples among the most impressive structures in the ancient world. Yet the empire's relationship with religious diversity was never simple, never static, and never purely doctrinal.

What follows examines how the Sasanian Empire managed - and sometimes mismanaged - the extraordinary religious plurality within its borders. Christians built churches in the shadow of fire temples. Jewish communities governed themselves under their own hereditary leaders. Manichaeans were hunted down with a ferocity reserved for few others. And the underlying logic - political far more than theological - determined who thrived and who suffered. What emerges is a portrait of an empire that was, by the standards of its age, surprisingly accommodating of difference, until difference became a threat to power.

Christians in a Zoroastrian Empire

Christianity arrived in Mesopotamia early - perhaps within a generation or two of the faith's founding - and by the time the Sasanians displaced the Parthians in 224 CE, Christian communities were already woven into the social fabric of the empire's western provinces.

For much of the early Sasanian period, these communities were tolerated. They were not equal citizens in any modern sense, and they operated under the watchful eye of Zoroastrian authorities, but they built churches, trained clergy, and maintained their own internal hierarchies. The Sasanian state, for all its investment in Zoroastrian orthodoxy, had little interest in expending energy on communities that paid their taxes, kept the peace, and caused no political trouble.

That calculus changed dramatically in the fourth century. When Constantine converted to Christianity in 312 CE and the Roman Empire began its own transformation into a Christian state, the religious identity of Persia's Christian minority acquired a new and dangerous political charge. From Shapur II's perspective, the Christians of his empire were now co-religionists of his most powerful enemy. Loyalty became suspect. Taxes became a test.

Shapur's response was a prolonged persecution that lasted, with varying intensity, across much of his reign. Christians were taxed at double the rate of other subjects - a punitive measure that was explicitly financial but carried a clear message about belonging. Those who refused or resisted faced harsher consequences. Clergy were targeted, churches were destroyed, and in some cases communities were forcibly relocated deeper into Persian territory, away from the Roman frontier where their loyalties might be acted upon.

Yet even this persecution had its limits and its logic. It was not a campaign to eradicate Christianity from the empire. It was a campaign to discipline a community that had become, through no fault of its own theology, a political liability. When the political context shifted - when Rome was no longer the immediate threat, or when a particular king needed Christian support - the pressure eased.

By the later Sasanian period, the relationship had transformed remarkably. The Church of the East, centered in the Sasanian-controlled city of Ctesiphon, developed into a significant institution. Some Sasanian kings came to see the Christian church not as a fifth column but as a useful counterweight to the power of the Zoroastrian clergy - a community that could provide administrative talent, diplomatic connections, and political loyalty precisely because it had no ties to Rome's now-rival church. Christianity, once a source of suspicion, had become, in certain contexts, an asset.

Jewish Communities and Autonomy

If Christians moved through the Sasanian world with considerable anxiety, the Jewish communities of Mesopotamia occupied a position of remarkable, if carefully bounded, stability.

Jews had lived in Mesopotamia since the Babylonian exile of the sixth century BCE - a presence stretching back over eight hundred years before the Sasanians came to power. By the third century CE, Mesopotamia was home to one of the largest and most intellectually vibrant Jewish communities in the world. The great academies of Sura and Pumbedita, established in this period, would eventually produce the Babylonian Talmud - one of the most consequential texts in Jewish history. This was not a community living in the margins. It was a community that had put down deep roots.

The Sasanian state accommodated this reality through a system of recognized communal autonomy. Jewish communities were governed internally by the Exilarch - the *Resh Galuta* - a hereditary leader who claimed descent from the Davidic line and who served as the official intermediary between the Jewish population and the imperial court.

This arrangement suited both sides. The Sasanians got a reliable mechanism for collecting taxes and maintaining order within Jewish communities without having to administer them directly. Jewish communities got a degree of self-governance that protected their religious and legal practices from direct interference.

This was not equality, and it was not without tension. Jews, like Christians, were subject to the authority of the Zoroastrian state and could not proselytize or challenge the social order. The Exilarch's position depended on maintaining good relations with the court, which meant that Jewish communal interests were always filtered through a figure who had his own political survival to consider. But within those constraints, the community functioned with a degree of autonomy that was, by the standards of the ancient world, genuinely significant.

Sasanian kings generally left Jewish communities alone as long as they remained politically quiescent and economically productive. Episodes of tension did arise - moments when a particular king or local official pushed harder against communal boundaries - but there was no sustained, empire-wide persecution of Jews in the Sasanian period comparable to what Christians experienced under Shapur II. The Jewish community's long establishment, its economic importance, and its lack of connection to any external rival power made it a far less threatening presence in the eyes of the throne.

Manichaeans and Persecution

Not every religious community in the Sasanian Empire found accommodation. The Manichaeans discovered, with brutal clarity, that the empire's tolerance had a ceiling - and that the ceiling was determined not by theology but by politics.

Manichaeism was founded by the prophet Mani, born in Mesopotamia around 216 CE. His teaching was a bold synthesis: drawing on Zoroastrian dualism, Christian scripture, and Buddhist concepts of enlightenment, Mani presented a universal religion that claimed to complete and supersede all previous revelations. He was, by all accounts, a figure of extraordinary charisma and intellectual ambition, and his faith spread rapidly across the empire and beyond.

For a brief period, Mani enjoyed royal favor. The early Sasanian king Shapur I appears to have found him interesting - perhaps useful as a counterweight to the growing power of the Zoroastrian priesthood, or perhaps simply as a curiosity worth patronizing. Mani traveled with the court and gained access to the empire's elites.

That window closed violently. Under Bahram I, the Zoroastrian high priest Kartir - a figure of immense institutional ambition who had spent decades consolidating clerical power - moved against Mani directly. Around 274 CE, Mani was arrested, tried, and executed. His followers were persecuted across the empire. Kartir's own inscriptions, carved into rock faces and still readable today, boast explicitly of his campaigns against heretics and religious minorities - Manichaeans, Christians, Buddhists, and others all named as targets.

What made the Manichaeans so threatening? Their universalism was part of it - a faith that claimed to supersede Zoroastrianism was an implicit challenge to the ideological foundations of Sasanian legitimacy. But the deeper issue was institutional. Manichaeism had no fixed territory, no ethnic base, no established community structure that the state could co-opt or control. It was a missionary faith that crossed borders and social classes with ease, and it had no Exilarch, no bishop tied to a specific city, no mechanism through which the state could manage it. In the blunt terms of political risk, it was ungovernable.

The persecution of Manichaeans continued intermittently across the Sasanian period. The faith survived - spreading westward into the Roman Empire and eastward along the Silk Roads into Central Asia and eventually China - but it never found a stable home within Persia itself.

Tolerance vs. Suppression

Laid side by side, the experiences of Christians, Jews, and Manichaeans reveal a pattern that has less to do with religious principle than with political calculus.

The Sasanian Empire was not a tolerant state in any idealistic sense. It did not protect minority religions out of a commitment to pluralism or freedom of conscience. What it practiced was something more pragmatic: a form of managed diversity, in which religious communities were permitted to exist as long as they could be made useful, controlled, or at least neutralized as threats.

Communities that had fixed addresses, recognized leaders, and established tax relationships with the state were manageable. Jews had the Exilarch. Christians, eventually, had their bishops and their catholicos in Ctesiphon. These structures gave the state handles - points of contact through which it could extract revenue, communicate demands, and hold communities accountable. Tolerance, in this framework, was essentially administrative.

Communities that lacked these structures, or whose beliefs made them inherently resistant to co-optation, faced a different fate. Manichaeans were persecuted not because Zoroastrian theology demanded it, but because they could not be managed. Their faith was transnational, their organization diffuse, and their implicit claim to universality was a direct challenge to the ideological order the Sasanian state depended upon.

Even Zoroastrianism itself was not immune to this logic. The Zoroastrian clergy - the Magi - were powerful precisely because they had made themselves indispensable to the state, providing ritual legitimacy for kings and administrative infrastructure for the empire. But that power was always contingent. Kings who felt the clergy had grown too strong sometimes patronized minority religions specifically to dilute clerical influence. Religion, in the Sasanian

Empire, was never above politics. It was always, in some essential sense, an instrument of it.

Religion as a Political Risk

The most revealing moments in Sasanian religious history are the ones where external politics and internal faith collided most directly.

Shapur II's persecution of Christians was the clearest example: a community that had lived quietly for generations became, almost overnight, a security concern because of events happening hundreds of miles away in Rome. The Christians themselves had not changed. Their theology had not changed. What had changed was the geopolitical context, and that was enough to transform them from tolerated subjects into suspected enemies.

This dynamic - in which the fate of a religious minority was determined less by what they believed than by who else believed it - recurred across the Sasanian period. The empire's long rivalry with Rome meant that any religious community with ties to the Roman world carried an inherent political risk. Conversely, communities that had no such ties, or that could be positioned as loyal alternatives to Roman-aligned groups, were sometimes actively cultivated.

By the late Sasanian period, the Church of the East had handled this reality with considerable sophistication. Having formally separated from the western churches at the Council of Seleucia-Ctesiphon in 410 CE, it could credibly present itself as a distinctly Persian institution - not a branch of Rome's church, but an independent tradition with its own theology, its own liturgical language, and its own political loyalties. That distinction helped it survive and, in some periods, flourish.

Religion in the Sasanian Empire was never just about salvation or ritual or the sacred. It was about belonging, loyalty, and power - about who could be trusted, who could be used, and who posed a threat that had to be contained.

Key Takeaways

- The Sasanian Empire was religiously diverse, home to Zoroastrians, Christians, Jews, Manichaeans, and others throughout its existence from 224 to 651 CE.

- Zoroastrianism was the official state religion, but Sasanian religious policy was driven primarily by political pragmatism rather than doctrinal conviction.

- Christians faced their most severe persecution under Shapur II in the fourth century - a response to Constantine's conversion and the political association between Christianity and Rome, not to Christian theology itself.

- Jewish communities enjoyed recognized autonomy through the institution of the Exilarch, making them administratively manageable and generally less subject to persecution.

- Manichaeans suffered the harshest and most sustained suppression, largely because their universalist, missionary faith could not be controlled through the administrative structures the state used to manage other communities.

- The Zoroastrian high priest Kartir played a central role in consolidating clerical power and directing persecution against religious minorities in the third century.

- By the later Sasanian period, the Church of the East had repositioned itself as a distinctly Persian institution, gaining political relevance as a counterweight to both Roman Christianity and the Zoroastrian clergy.

- Tolerance and suppression in the Sasanian Empire were not fixed policies but shifting responses to political circumstances - determined above all by whether a religious community could be managed, used, or neutralized.

Empires rarely survive by force alone. The Sasanian state endured for over four centuries in part because it found ways to incorporate diversity without being destabilized by it - not through idealism, but through a hard-nosed recognition that millions of subjects who were not Zoroastrian still had to be governed, taxed, and kept from rebellion. That the system was imperfect, sometimes brutal, and always self-serving does not make it less historically significant. What the Sasanians built was a working template for managing religious plurality under imperial rule - one that later empires, including the Islamic caliphates that eventually succeeded them, would study, adapt, and in some ways refine. How that succession unfolded, and what it meant for the diverse communities that had lived under Sasanian rule for centuries, is a story that awaits its own telling.

Chapter 9:
Life in the Empire

Empires are built by rulers, but lived by ordinary people.

Behind every military campaign, every royal decree, every shift in dynastic power, there were farmers rising before dawn, merchants haggling in crowded bazaars, priests tending sacred fires, and mothers teaching children the prayers that had been spoken for generations. The Sasanian Empire, which stretched from the Euphrates to the Oxus and endured for more than four centuries, was not simply a political structure. It was a civilization - layered, complex, and deeply human.

We know the names of kings. We know the dates of battles. But what did it actually feel like to live inside this empire? What determined whether a person rose or struggled? What shaped the rhythms of a day, the structure of a family, the texture of a life? Those questions are harder to answer, and far more interesting.

This chapter turns away from the throne room and toward the street, the field, the household, and the marketplace. It examines the social order that governed who held power and who did not, the family structures that anchored daily existence, the sharp differences between city and countryside, and the inequalities that ran like fault lines beneath the empire's gleaming surface. And it asks, finally, what it meant - in any meaningful sense - to be Sasanian.

Social Classes and Hierarchy

Order was not merely a preference in the Sasanian world. It was a theology.

Sasanian society was organized according to a rigidly defined system of estates, each with its own role, its own obligations, and its own place in the cosmic order. This hierarchy was not incidental to

Zoroastrian belief - it was embedded in it. The idea that the world functioned properly when each person fulfilled their appointed station gave the social structure a religious legitimacy that made it both powerful and remarkably durable.

At the apex stood the king of kings - the *shahanshah* - whose authority was understood as divinely sanctioned. Below him, the empire's social order was divided into four broad estates: the priests, the warriors, the scribes and administrators, and the artisans and farmers. These were not merely occupational categories. They were hereditary identities, carrying with them specific rights, duties, and expectations that passed from parent to child across generations.

The Priestly Class

The Zoroastrian clergy - the *magi* - occupied a position of immense prestige and institutional power. They were the guardians of the sacred fires, the interpreters of divine law, and the administrators of religious ritual that touched every aspect of life, from birth to death. Their influence extended well beyond the temple. Priests advised rulers, managed significant landholdings, and served as the ideological backbone of the empire's claim to legitimacy. Zoroastrianism was the state religion, and the clergy who maintained it were among the most powerful figures in the land.

The Warrior Nobility

Just below the priests in formal prestige - and arguably their rivals in real-world power - stood the warrior aristocracy. These were the great noble families, the *azadan* and the higher-ranking *wuzurgan*, who controlled vast estates, commanded armies, and governed provinces. Their loyalty was essential to any king who wished to rule effectively. When that loyalty fractured, as it periodically did, the consequences could be catastrophic. The Sasanian court was never entirely free from the threat of aristocratic rebellion, and several kings discovered this at great personal cost.

Scribes, Administrators, and the Educated Middle

The third estate - scribes, bureaucrats, and administrators - occupied a curious middle position. They lacked the hereditary glamour of the warrior nobility and the sacred authority of the priests, but the empire could not function without them. Literacy, record-keeping, tax collection, legal administration - these were the unglamorous machinery of imperial governance, and the men who managed them wielded quiet but genuine influence. Some rose to positions of considerable power through competence and royal favor, moving through a world where talent occasionally trumped birth.

Artisans, Farmers, and the Laboring Majority

At the base of the formal hierarchy stood the vast majority of the empire's population: farmers, craftsmen, traders, and laborers. They were not without dignity in the Zoroastrian worldview - productive labor was considered virtuous, and agriculture in particular was seen as a sacred act, the cultivation of Ahura Mazda's good creation. But dignity in theory did not always translate into comfort in practice. This was the estate that fed the empire, built its cities, and filled its armies - and it was also the estate that bore the heaviest burden of taxation.

Beyond the Four Estates

The formal hierarchy did not capture everyone. The Sasanian Empire was religiously diverse in ways that complicated the neat social picture. Significant communities of Jews, Christians, and Manicheans lived within imperial borders, each with their own internal hierarchies, their own institutions, and their own complicated relationships with Zoroastrian authority. Christians, in particular, occupied an ambiguous position - sometimes tolerated, sometimes persecuted, their status shifting with the political winds and the empire's relationship with Rome, where Christianity had become the state religion.

Family Structures and Daily Rhythms

If the estate system defined a person's place in the world, the family defined their experience of it day to day.

The household was the fundamental unit of Sasanian life. Extended family networks provided economic support, social identity, and protection in a world where the state's reach was often limited and personal connections were the most reliable form of security. A person's family determined not only their social standing but their occupation, their marriage prospects, and the religious practices that structured their days.

Marriage was arranged, typically within social groups, and carried significant legal and economic weight. Zoroastrian law recognized several categories of marriage, with the primary wife holding a distinct legal status that affected inheritance and the legitimacy of children. Households could be large and multigenerational, with grandparents, parents, children, and sometimes more distant relatives sharing space, resources, and responsibility.

The Shape of a Day

Daily life for most Sasanians was organized around the rhythms of work, prayer, and seasonal obligation. For the farming majority, the day began early - before sunrise in the planting and harvest seasons - and revolved around the demands of the land. Zoroastrian practice wove prayer into the structure of the day itself, with specific devotional moments tied to the five divisions of the day recognized in religious tradition. Fire, as the sacred symbol of Ahura Mazda's presence, was tended carefully in the household hearth as well as in the great temple fires maintained by the clergy.

Food was simple for most people: bread, legumes, dairy, and seasonal vegetables formed the staple diet, supplemented by meat for those who could afford it. Shared meals carried social and religious significance - hospitality was a virtue deeply embedded in Persian culture, and the table was a space where relationships were maintained and obligations honored.

Children entered the world of adult responsibility early. Boys from noble or priestly families might receive formal education in religious texts or administrative skills. For most children, however, education meant apprenticeship - learning the trade, the craft, or the farming practice of their parents through observation and labor.

Rural vs. Urban Experience

To speak of "life in the Sasanian Empire" as a single experience is to flatten a reality that was, in fact, sharply divided by geography.

The empire's cities - Ctesiphon above all, the great imperial capital on the Tigris - were worlds unto themselves. Ctesiphon was among the largest cities in the ancient world during the Sasanian period, a sprawling complex of palaces, markets, workshops, and neighborhoods that drew merchants, artisans, diplomats, and migrants from across the known world. The famous *Taq Kasra*, the great arched hall of the Sasanian palace, stood as a monument to imperial ambition visible for miles.

Urban life meant proximity to power, access to trade, and exposure to the empire's remarkable cultural diversity. Merchants from the Roman world, Central Asia, India, and Arabia passed through Sasanian cities, carrying goods and ideas. Workshops produced fine textiles, metalwork, and glassware that traveled along trade routes stretching far beyond the empire's borders. For those with the right connections and skills, the city offered opportunities unavailable anywhere else.

The Countryside

For the majority of the empire's population, however, the city was a distant reality. Rural life was defined by agriculture - the cultivation of wheat, barley, and other crops in the river valleys and irrigated plains that formed the empire's agricultural heartland. The Sasanians invested significantly in irrigation infrastructure, and the management of water was both an economic and a political concern. Canals and *qanats* - underground water channels - made agriculture possible in regions that would otherwise have been too arid to farm.

Village communities were largely self-sufficient and tightly knit. Local landowners - often members of the lesser nobility - exercised considerable authority over the peasants who worked their estates, collecting rents and dues that flowed upward through the imperial tax system. The relationship between landlord and peasant was not always exploitative by design, but the structural inequality built into it meant that rural life offered little room for upward mobility.

Distance from the capital also meant distance from the empire's cultural and intellectual life. Theological debates, artistic patronage, the cosmopolitan exchange of ideas - these were largely urban phenomena. Rural communities maintained their own traditions, their own local religious practices, and their own rhythms, connected to the broader empire primarily through taxation, military conscription, and the occasional visit of an imperial official.

Wealth, Poverty, and Inequality

The Sasanian Empire produced extraordinary wealth. It also produced extraordinary poverty. These two facts were not unrelated.

At the top of the economic pyramid, the great noble families controlled vast agricultural estates, benefited from trade revenues, and accumulated luxury goods - fine silks, silver plate, elaborate jewelry - that signaled their status and reinforced their power. The royal court at Ctesiphon was legendary for its opulence, and the *shahanshah* himself was expected to display wealth on a scale that communicated divine favor and imperial dominance.

Below the nobility, a middling layer of merchants, skilled craftsmen, and lesser administrators occupied an economically varied but often precarious position. Trade could generate significant wealth, but it was also subject to disruption - war, shifting political alliances, and the unpredictable demands of imperial taxation could undermine a merchant's livelihood with little warning.

The Weight of Taxation

For the farming majority, taxation was the most direct and tangible expression of imperial power. Land taxes and poll taxes formed the backbone of imperial revenue, and their burden fell most heavily on those least able to bear it. Periods of military expansion or costly warfare - and the Sasanian Empire experienced both frequently - often led to increased fiscal pressure on rural communities. When harvests failed or tax collectors arrived with impossible demands, the consequences could be devastating.

Debt, displacement, and dependency were recurring features of life at the lower end of the economic scale. Some peasants fell into forms of bound labor that limited their freedom of movement and tied them to the land and its owners. The gap between the empire's wealthiest and its poorest inhabitants was not merely economic - it was a chasm that shaped every aspect of daily experience, from diet and housing to legal rights and life expectancy.

What It Meant to Be Sasanian

Identity in the ancient world was rarely simple, and Sasanian identity was no exception.

To be Sasanian was, in one sense, to participate in a civilization that understood itself as the rightful heir to a long Persian tradition - a tradition that the dynasty's founders had deliberately invoked when they overthrew the Parthians and set about what historians have called the "Iranization" of culture. They pulled away from the Hellenistic influences of earlier centuries and reasserted Zoroastrian religion and Persian language as the foundations of imperial life. This was a conscious project of cultural identity-building, and it left deep marks on art, architecture, literature, and law.

But the empire was also genuinely diverse. Jews maintained their communities and their traditions. Christians built churches. Manicheans, despite periodic persecution, preserved their faith. Merchants from distant lands brought foreign customs and foreign gods. The Sasanian world was not monolithic - it was a mosaic, held together by imperial authority, shared economic networks, and the overarching framework of Zoroastrian state religion, but never fully homogenized.

For most ordinary people, identity was probably experienced less as an abstract allegiance to "the empire" and more as a web of immediate loyalties - to family, to village, to local lord, to the fire temple down the road. The grand narrative of Sasanian civilization was real, but it was lived in small, specific, human ways: in the prayers spoken at dawn, the bread broken at a shared table, the craft passed from parent to child, the fire kept burning through the night.

Quick Summary

- Sasanian society was organized into four hereditary estates - priests, warriors, scribes, and farmers - each with defined roles rooted in Zoroastrian cosmology.

- The Zoroastrian clergy held immense institutional power, while the warrior nobility controlled land and military force; tension between these groups shaped imperial politics.

- The family was the central unit of daily life, providing economic support, social identity, and religious structure across generations.

- Urban centers like Ctesiphon were cosmopolitan hubs of trade and culture, while the rural majority lived in largely self-sufficient agricultural communities.

- Sasanian irrigation infrastructure - including *qanats* and canal systems - made large-scale agriculture possible and was central to imperial wealth.

- Wealth was highly concentrated among the nobility and royal court, while heavy taxation fell disproportionately on farmers and the laboring majority.

- The empire was religiously diverse, with significant Jewish, Christian, and Manichean communities existing alongside the Zoroastrian majority.

- Sasanian identity was shaped by a deliberate cultural project of "Iranization," but was experienced by most people through immediate, local loyalties rather than grand imperial allegiance.

Four centuries is a long time for any civilization to endure, and the Sasanian Empire endured not simply because of its armies or its kings, but because it gave millions of ordinary people a framework for living - a social order, a spiritual vocabulary, a set of daily practices that made the world legible and life meaningful. When that empire finally fell in 651 CE, it was not just a dynasty that ended. A whole way of life began its long transformation into something new, something shaped by the arrival of Islam and the remaking of the entire Near East. The world those ordinary Sasanians had built - in their fields, their households, their fire temples, and their markets - would leave traces that outlasted the empire itself by centuries.

Chapter 10:
Women and Gender in the Sasanian World

She left no name in the chronicles. No court poet celebrated her. No silver plate bears her image riding to the hunt or receiving tribute from conquered peoples. Yet she was there - managing a household, negotiating a marriage contract, perhaps overseeing agricultural land in her own name, raising children who would one day serve the empire's armies or temples. For every queen whose name survived in a royal inscription, thousands of women moved through the Sasanian world in near-total historical silence.

That silence is itself a kind of evidence. It tells us something about who the Sasanian Empire considered worth recording, and who it did not. The empire that ruled Iran and much of the ancient Near East from 224 to 651 CE was one of the most sophisticated political and cultural entities of late antiquity. Its legal codes were elaborate, its religious institutions powerful, its artistic traditions rich. Yet when modern historians try to reconstruct the lives of women within it, they find themselves working against the grain of sources designed, almost entirely, by men for men.

What survives - Zoroastrian juridical texts, royal inscriptions, seal impressions, silver plate iconography, and scattered references in foreign chronicles - offers fragments rather than portraits. But fragments, read carefully, can be remarkably revealing. They show a society that was patriarchal in its assumptions and hierarchical in its structures, but also one in which women exercised real legal rights, wielded genuine political influence, and participated meaningfully in religious life. The picture that emerges is neither simple oppression nor hidden equality. It is something more complicated, and more human, than either.

Legal Status and Property Rights

Sasanian law was not a casual affair. Rooted in Zoroastrian religious tradition and codified in texts known as the *Mādayān ī Hazār Dādestān* - the "Book of a Thousand Judgments" - it governed everything from inheritance disputes to the terms of marriage contracts with a degree of precision that would have impressed a Roman jurist. Within this legal architecture, women occupied a defined, if constrained, position.

Women in Sasanian Iran could own property. This was not a minor concession. In a world where legal personhood often tracked closely with economic independence, the right to hold land, goods, and assets in one's own name gave women a form of social standing that pure domestic subordination would not have allowed. Juridical texts confirm that women could enter into contracts, manage estates, and conduct business - capacities that imply a practical engagement with economic life well beyond the household threshold.

Marriage law, however, reveals the patriarchal logic underlying these rights. Sasanian legal texts distinguished between different categories of wives, with the *pādixšāy* wife - the fully authorized, primary wife - holding the highest legal status. Her children were legitimate heirs; her position within the household carried formal recognition. Secondary wives and concubines occupied lower rungs of a carefully stratified system. The texts make clear that the purpose of marriage, in legal terms, was fundamentally about producing male heirs. Family continuity meant male continuity. A woman's reproductive role was not incidental to her legal status - it was central to it.

This emphasis on male lineage shaped the law in revealing ways. Juridical texts consistently placed men in superior positions in legal disputes, particularly those involving inheritance and guardianship. A woman, even one with property rights, typically required a male guardian - a father, husband, or designated representative - to act in certain legal capacities on her behalf. The law acknowledged her personhood while simultaneously circumscribing her autonomy.

What this created was a system of partial rights - real enough to matter in daily life, limited enough to reinforce the broader social hierarchy. A widow managing her late husband's estate, a merchant's wife overseeing trade goods in his absence, a landowner negotiating a lease: all of these figures are plausible within Sasanian legal norms. None of them operated as fully independent agents in the modern sense. They moved within a framework that granted them room to act while ensuring that room remained bounded.

The law was not designed to liberate women. But it was also not designed to render them invisible. That distinction matters.

Elite Women: Queens, Mothers, and Power Brokers

If ordinary women left few traces, elite women - queens, royal mothers, and aristocratic figures - left rather more. Not always by name, and not always in flattering terms, but enough to suggest that at the highest levels of Sasanian society, women could exercise influence that went well beyond ceremonial presence.

Royal women occupied a structurally significant position in the Sasanian court. The queen mother, in particular, held a role that combined symbolic authority with practical leverage. In a dynasty where succession was frequently contested and royal sons competed fiercely for the throne, a king's mother could be a crucial political actor - managing alliances, supporting her son's claim, and steering the dangerous currents of court politics with considerable skill. The sources rarely describe this work in detail, but its effects are visible in the patterns of succession and patronage that shaped the dynasty's history.

Sasanian silver plate - one of the richest visual sources for the empire - offers a striking glimpse of how elite women were imagined, if not always how they actually lived. Hunting scenes dominate the royal iconography, and they are almost exclusively male. Kings ride, shoot, and triumph. Women appear at the margins: as attendants, as figures in banquet scenes, occasionally as musicians. The visual language of power was masculine by design. Yet the very existence of female figures in court art, however subordinate their depicted roles, confirms that women were present in the elite spaces these images celebrated.

Some Sasanian queens achieved a visibility that the artistic conventions of their time rarely granted women. Foreign sources - Byzantine chronicles, Armenian histories - occasionally mention Sasanian royal women in contexts that suggest genuine political agency. A queen interceding with her husband on behalf of a foreign embassy, a royal mother whose preferences shaped the selection of an heir: these are glimpses, not portraits, but they are glimpses of real power operating through the channels available to women in a patriarchal court.

Aristocratic women below the royal family also participated in networks of patronage and influence. Seal impressions - small, personal objects used to authenticate documents and correspondence - survive in significant numbers from the Sasanian period, and a meaningful proportion of them belonged to women. A woman with her own seal was a woman conducting her own business, managing her own affairs, leaving her own mark on the documentary record. That these seals exist at all is a quiet but important corrective to any picture of total female passivity.

Elite women, then, were not merely ornamental. They were actors in a political and social world that officially privileged men, finding leverage where the system allowed it and sometimes where it did not.

Women in Religious Life

Zoroastrianism - the faith that gave the Sasanian Empire much of its ideological backbone - had a complicated relationship with gender. Its cosmology and ritual life were deeply patriarchal. The priesthood, the *magi*, was male. Religious authority flowed through male lineages. The great theological texts were composed by men and addressed, in the main, to male concerns.

Yet Zoroastrianism did not exclude women from religious participation. Women could attend and participate in religious ceremonies. The faith's emphasis on purity, on the maintenance of cosmic order through correct ritual behavior, applied to women as well as men - which meant that women had religious obligations, and with obligations came a form of religious standing. A woman who maintained the sacred fire, who observed the ritual purity laws, who raised her children in the faith, was performing acts of genuine religious significance.

The purity laws themselves reveal the ambivalence at the heart of Zoroastrian gender thinking. Menstruating women were considered ritually impure and were subject to specific restrictions - separated from the household, prohibited from certain activities, required to undergo purification before returning to normal life. These practices reflected a broader anxiety about female bodies and their relationship to the sacred. They also imposed real constraints on women's daily lives and movements.

Purity was not only a burden, however. It was also a form of significance. A woman who correctly observed the purity laws was actively maintaining the cosmic order that Zoroastrianism placed at the center of its worldview. Her compliance was not passive - it was a form of religious labor, recognized as such by the tradition.

Zoroastrian texts also addressed women's spiritual fate. Women, like men, were understood to have souls that would face judgment after death. The faith's eschatology did not consign women to a lesser afterlife by virtue of their sex. This theological equality of souls coexisted, somewhat uneasily, with the social and ritual inequalities of earthly life - a tension that Zoroastrian thinkers did not always resolve cleanly.

What emerges from the religious evidence is a picture of inclusion that was real but bounded. Women were part of the Zoroastrian community in meaningful ways. They were not, however, equal participants in its formal structures of authority.

Ordinary Women: Work, Family, and Agency

Step back from the queens and the legal codes, and the question becomes harder: what did daily life actually look like for the vast majority of Sasanian women - the farmers, the weavers, the merchants' wives, the servants?

Here the evidence thins dramatically. Archaeology offers some help. Textile production, almost universally associated with women across ancient societies, was clearly a major economic activity in the Sasanian world. Loom weights, spindle whorls, and the evidence of sophisticated weaving traditions suggest that women's labor was central to household and perhaps commercial textile production. This was not marginal work. Textiles were valuable goods, and the women who produced them were contributing to household economies in ways that mattered.

Agricultural communities, which formed the backbone of the Sasanian economy, almost certainly relied on women's labor in fields and orchards as well as in domestic spaces. The sharp division between "public" male work and "private" female work that later ideologies would impose was probably less rigid in practice than in theory, particularly in rural settings where survival demanded flexibility.

Family life structured most women's experience. Marriage, childbearing, and the management of the household were the primary social roles that Sasanian society assigned to women, and for most women, these roles consumed most of their lives. But within those roles, there was room for agency - in the negotiation of marriage terms, in the management of household resources, in the raising of children who would carry the family's future.

The evidence does not allow confident reconstruction of individual lives. But it resists, firmly, any reading of ordinary Sasanian women as purely passive or powerless. They worked, they managed, they negotiated. They did so within constraints that were real and sometimes severe. They did so nonetheless.

What the Evidence Tells Us - and What It Doesn't

Any honest account of women in the Sasanian world has to reckon with the limits of what we can know. The sources are sparse, skewed, and almost entirely produced by men. Legal texts tell us what the law said, not how it was applied or evaded. Royal art tells us how the elite wanted to be seen, not how women actually lived within those courts. Foreign chronicles filtered Sasanian reality through their own cultural assumptions.

What the evidence does tell us is this: Sasanian women existed within a patriarchal system that assigned them subordinate legal status while granting them real, if limited, rights. Elite women could exercise genuine political influence through the informal channels available to them. Religious life included women as participants, if not as leaders. Ordinary women's labor was economically essential, even when it was socially invisible.

What the evidence does not tell us is how women themselves understood their lives - what they valued, what they resisted, what they hoped for. Their inner lives are almost entirely lost. The silences in the record are not neutral. They reflect choices made, over centuries, about whose experiences were worth preserving.

Recovering those experiences, even partially, is not merely an academic exercise. The Sasanian Empire's gender structures left traces in the societies that followed it, including the early Islamic world that absorbed much of its legal and social inheritance. Understanding how gender worked in this empire - its contradictions, its compromises, its moments of unexpected agency - is part of understanding how the ancient world shaped the world that came after.

Quick Summary

- Sasanian women held legal rights to property ownership and could enter contracts, but operated within a patriarchal framework that emphasized male lineage and required male guardianship in many legal contexts.

- Marriage law was hierarchical, distinguishing between primary and secondary wives, with a woman's reproductive role central to her legal standing.

- Elite women - particularly queen mothers and aristocratic figures - exercised real political influence through informal channels, even when formal power remained male.

- Seal impressions belonging to women confirm that at least some women conducted their own affairs and participated in the documentary culture of the empire.

- Zoroastrianism included women in religious life and assigned their souls equal spiritual standing, while simultaneously imposing ritual restrictions tied to female purity.

- Ordinary women's labor in textile production, agriculture, and household management was economically essential, even when it went unrecorded.

- The historical record is sparse and male-dominated; recovering women's experiences requires reading against the grain of sources not designed to preserve them.

- Sasanian gender structures influenced the early Islamic societies that succeeded the empire, making their study relevant beyond the empire's own historical period.

The women of the Sasanian world were neither the passive figures that official ideology preferred nor the hidden heroines that modern romanticism might wish them to be. They were people who moved through a system that constrained them in some ways and accommodated them in others - finding room to act, to own, to worship, and to matter, within the limits their world imposed. That those limits were real should not obscure the fact that the room within them was real too. History has been slow to look for them. The looking, at last, is underway.

Part 4
War, Diplomacy, and Global Power

Chapter 11:
Rome vs. Persia - The Endless War

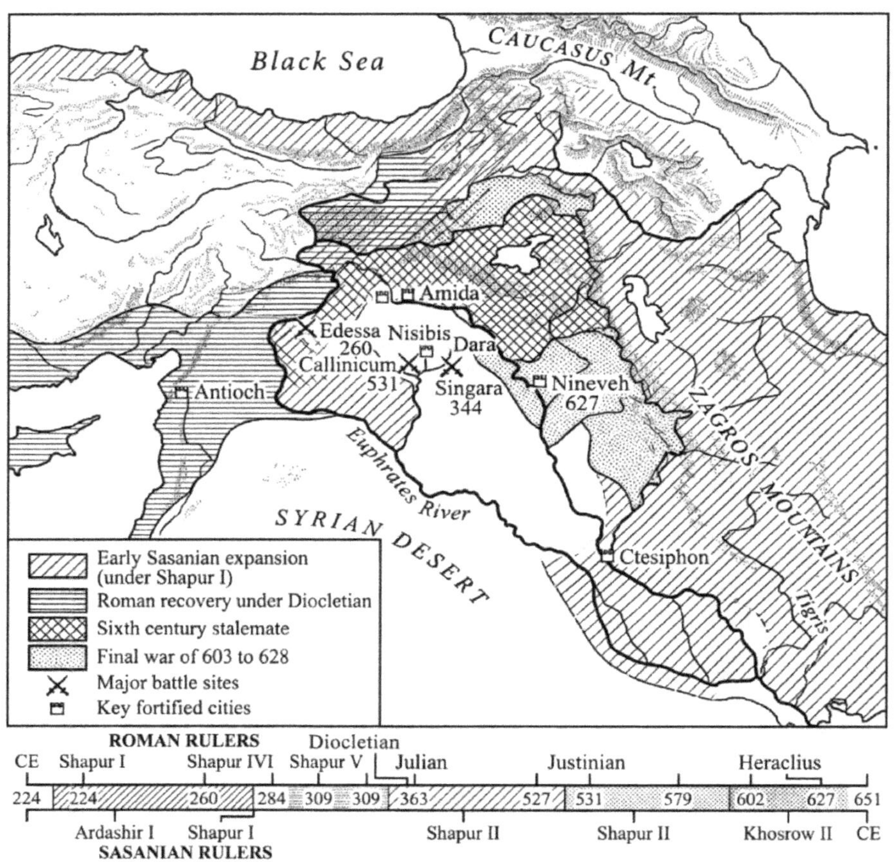

Four Centuries of Conflict:
The Roman-Persian Frontier (230–630 CE)

In the summer of 627 CE, a Roman army marched deep into Persian territory and met its enemy near the ruins of ancient Nineveh. What followed was not just a battle - it was the final act of a rivalry that had consumed two civilizations for the better part of seven centuries.

A Conflict Older Than the Empire Itself

Most people think of Rome's great enemies as the Germanic tribes who eventually brought the Western Empire to its knees, or perhaps Carthage, whose general Hannibal once camped within sight of Rome's walls. But neither of those rivalries lasted more than a few generations. The contest between Rome and Persia was something different entirely - a sustained, grinding, generational struggle that outlasted dynasties, religions, and entire political systems.

From roughly the third century BCE, when Rome was still consolidating its grip on the Italian peninsula, through to the seventh century CE, the eastern frontier was never truly at peace. Persia - first under the Parthian dynasty, then under the Sasanians - stood as the one power in the ancient world that Rome could never simply conquer, absorb, or intimidate into submission. Two empires, two visions of civilization, two systems of power: and between them, a borderland that both sides bled for, generation after generation, without either ever winning for good.

What follows traces that rivalry from its origins to its exhausted conclusion - the wars that defined it, the strategies that shaped it, the costs it imposed, and the strange equilibrium it ultimately produced.

Origins of the Rivalry

Rome and Persia did not begin as natural enemies. For much of the early Republican period, Persia - in the form of the Achaemenid Empire - was a distant presence, a power that had clashed with the Greeks but had little direct contact with Rome. Alexander the Great destroyed the Achaemenid dynasty in the 330s BCE, and for a time, the successor kingdoms he left behind formed a buffer between the Mediterranean world and the Iranian plateau.

That changed when the Parthians rose to power in the third century BCE. Emerging from the steppes of Central Asia, the Parthian dynasty gradually consolidated control over Iran and Mesopotamia, and by the first century BCE, they had pushed their frontier westward to the Euphrates River - directly into territory Rome considered its own sphere of influence.

The collision was almost inevitable. Rome was expanding eastward, absorbing the remnants of Alexander's empire, drawing client kingdoms into its orbit. Persia, under the Parthians, was doing the same from the other direction. The Euphrates became the fault line between two tectonic plates of power.

Early encounters were humbling for Rome. In 53 BCE, the Roman general Crassus - one of the wealthiest men in the Republic and a member of the ruling triumvirate alongside Caesar and Pompey - led an army into Parthian territory and was annihilated at the Battle of Carrhae. Thousands of Roman soldiers were killed or captured; Crassus himself died in the aftermath. It was one of the worst defeats in Roman military history, and it announced clearly that Persia would not be easily brushed aside.

Yet Rome kept trying. Julius Caesar was reportedly planning a major eastern campaign when he was assassinated in 44 BCE. Mark Antony launched an invasion of Parthia in 36 BCE that ended in costly retreat. Emperor Trajan pushed deep into Mesopotamia in the early second century CE, briefly capturing the Parthian capital of Ctesiphon - only for his gains to unravel almost immediately after his death.

A pattern was forming. Rome could win battles, even major ones. It could seize cities and territory. But it could not hold the east. Persia, for its part, could resist and counterattack, but it could not push Rome back to the Mediterranean. Each side was strong enough to deny the other total victory, but neither was strong enough to achieve it.

When the Sasanian dynasty overthrew the Parthians in 224 CE, the rivalry intensified rather than reset. The Sasanians were more aggressive, more centralized, and more ideologically motivated than their predecessors. They saw themselves as heirs to the ancient Achaemenid Empire - the empire Alexander had destroyed - and they wanted their territory back. That meant direct confrontation with Rome on a scale the Parthians had rarely attempted.

Key Wars and Turning Points

Over seven centuries, the Roman-Persian conflict produced dozens of wars, campaigns, and skirmishes. A few stand out as genuine turning points.

The Iberian War (526-532 CE) began as a dispute over the kingdom of Iberia - modern Georgia - caught between the two empires. Roman Emperor Justin I and Persian King Kavadh I both claimed influence over the region, and when Iberia's king sought Roman protection against Persian pressure, war followed. The conflict was inconclusive militarily, but it set the template for the later, far more destructive wars of the sixth and seventh centuries: proxy kingdoms, disputed buffer zones, and the constant friction of two powers who could not agree on where one empire ended and the other began.

The war of 572-591 CE proved more decisive, at least temporarily. Persia suffered significant military setbacks, and internal instability - including civil conflict that weakened the Persian state from within - forced a peace settlement that favored Rome. For a brief moment, it seemed the balance might finally tip.

It didn't. The wars resumed, and by the early seventh century, the conflict had reached its most catastrophic phase. The Sasanian Empire launched a massive offensive that overran Roman Syria, Palestine, and Egypt - territories Rome had held for centuries. Jerusalem fell. Alexandria fell. Persian armies reached the Bosphorus, within sight of Constantinople itself. It was the closest either side had ever come to total victory.

Rome's response, under Emperor Heraclius, was one of the most dramatic reversals in ancient military history. Heraclius reorganized his forces, secured alliances, and launched a series of deep counteroffensives into Persian territory. He bypassed the obvious routes, struck where the Persians were vulnerable, and kept the initiative.

The Battle of Nineveh in 627 CE was the culmination of that campaign. Near the ruins of the ancient Assyrian capital, Roman forces defeated the Persian army in a decisive engagement. Historian Farid Rad has described it as the final significant Roman victory in the long conflict - and the numbers bear that out. The Persian court descended into chaos. King Khosrow II, who had overseen the great Persian conquests, was overthrown and killed by his own son. The empire that had nearly destroyed Rome was suddenly tearing itself apart.

Peace followed. Rome recovered most of what it had lost. But neither side had the strength left to press further.

Strategy and Objectives

What were these two empires actually fighting for? The answer is more complicated than simple conquest.

Territory mattered, but not in the way modern readers might expect. Neither Rome nor Persia genuinely believed it could absorb the other entirely. The distances were too great, the logistics too difficult, the cultural differences too deep. What both sides fought for, repeatedly, was control of the borderlands - the rich agricultural regions of Mesopotamia, the trade routes connecting the Mediterranean to Central Asia and India, and the buffer kingdoms like Armenia and Iberia that sat between the two empires.

Control of these zones meant revenue, prestige, and strategic depth. Losing them meant vulnerability. So both empires spent enormous resources fighting over territories that neither could permanently hold.

A powerful element of ideology reinforced the competition. Rome saw itself as the universal empire, the civilizing force of the known world. Persia, especially under the Sasanians, saw itself as the rightful heir to a great imperial tradition stretching back to Cyrus and Darius. Neither could fully accept the other's legitimacy. Every peace treaty was, in some sense, a temporary truce - a pause before the next round.

Military strategy on both sides reflected these realities. Rome relied on its disciplined infantry, its engineering capacity - roads, fortifications, supply lines - and its ability to project force across vast distances. Persia countered with heavy cavalry, mobile warfare, and a deep strategic reserve in the Iranian plateau that Rome could threaten but never truly conquer. Neither side's strengths could fully neutralize the other's.

The Cost of Endless Conflict

Seven centuries of war leaves marks that go far beyond the battlefield.

The human cost was staggering. Armies numbered in the tens of thousands; battles killed thousands in a single day. But the civilian toll was often worse. Mesopotamia, the Levant, and Anatolia were fought over repeatedly, their cities sacked, their populations displaced or enslaved, their agricultural systems disrupted. Regions that had been prosperous for centuries were periodically reduced to ruin.

The financial cost was equally severe. Both empires spent enormous sums maintaining their frontier armies, building and rebuilding fortifications, and subsidizing client kingdoms. Rome's eastern legions were among the most expensive military commitments in the empire's budget. Persia maintained comparable forces on its western frontier. Neither could fully redirect those resources elsewhere -

which meant that both empires were perpetually constrained in what they could do on their other frontiers.

A deeper cost, harder to quantify, accompanied the material losses. Constant warfare shapes institutions, cultures, and political systems in ways that outlast any individual conflict. Both Rome and Persia developed highly militarized frontier societies, with powerful generals who sometimes used their armies to make or unmake emperors. The instability this created - coups, civil wars, succession crises - was itself partly a product of the endless eastern war.

By the time the Battle of Nineveh was fought in 627 CE, both empires were exhausted in ways that went beyond troop numbers or treasury balances. They had been fighting, in various forms, for longer than most modern nations have existed.

Stalemate and Balance of Power

Perhaps the most striking feature of the Roman-Persian conflict is not how much it changed, but how little.

After seven centuries of war, the frontier between the two empires ran, roughly, where it had always run - along the Euphrates and through the Armenian highlands. Neither side had achieved permanent dominance. Neither had been destroyed. The wars had produced enormous suffering and consumed incalculable resources, but the fundamental balance of power had barely shifted.

This was not an accident. Both empires had developed, through long experience, a kind of strategic equilibrium - an understanding of what was achievable and what was not. Rome knew it could not hold Mesopotamia permanently. Persia knew it could not push to the Mediterranean. Each side could hurt the other; neither could finish it.

What ended the conflict was not a Roman victory or a Persian one. It was the arrival of a third force that neither empire had anticipated. Within a decade of the Battle of Nineveh, Arab armies carrying the new faith of Islam swept out of the Arabian Peninsula and shattered both empires simultaneously. Persia collapsed entirely. Rome - by then the Byzantine Empire - survived, but lost Egypt, Syria, and Palestine permanently.

The endless war between Rome and Persia had, in a grim irony, helped create the conditions for its own termination. Both empires were too weakened, too financially drained, and too politically unstable after centuries of mutual destruction to resist the new force rising from the south. The stalemate that had defined their relationship for seven centuries ended not with one side winning, but with both sides losing to someone else entirely.

Quick Summary

- Rome and Persia fought, in various forms, for roughly seven centuries - from the late Republican period through the early seventh century CE.

- The rivalry began when the Parthian Empire expanded westward to the Euphrates, placing it in direct competition with Rome's eastern ambitions.

- The Sasanian dynasty, which replaced the Parthians in 224 CE, intensified the conflict with a more aggressive and ideologically driven foreign policy.

- Key flashpoints included the Iberian War (526-532 CE), the war of 572-591 CE in which Persia suffered significant defeats, and the catastrophic seventh-century campaigns that nearly destroyed both empires.

- The Battle of Nineveh in 627 CE was the final decisive Roman victory, triggering a Persian civil war and forcing a peace settlement.

- Despite centuries of warfare, neither side achieved permanent territorial dominance - the frontier remained roughly where it had always been.

- Both empires were so weakened by their mutual conflict that they could not resist the Arab conquests of the 630s and 640s CE, which ended the rivalry by destroying one participant and permanently diminishing the other.

The Roman-Persian wars stand as one of history's most instructive examples of what happens when two great powers are evenly matched and neither can afford to stop fighting. They bled each other for generations, achieved no lasting resolution, and in the end left both civilizations vulnerable to a transformation neither had seen coming. What the sword could not settle, history settled in its own way - and the world that emerged from the ruins looked nothing like either empire had imagined.

Chapter 12:

The Sasanian War Machine

Imagine a wall of iron moving toward you across the open plain. Not a wall of shields - a wall of men and horses, both armored head to hoof in overlapping steel plates, moving at a controlled canter that shakes the ground beneath your feet. No gap to exploit. No weak point to target. Just the slow, grinding advance of something that seems less like an army and more like a force of nature.

This was the *clibanarius* - the Sasanian super-heavy cavalryman - and for over four centuries, he was the most feared soldier on the western face of the ancient world.

An Empire Built on Horseback

When Ardashir I overthrew the Parthian king Artabanus IV in AD 224 and founded the Sasanian dynasty, he inherited more than a throne. He inherited a military tradition stretching back centuries - one that placed the horse at the center of Persian power. What the Sasanians did with that tradition, however, was something new. Over the following four centuries, they built a war machine of remarkable sophistication, one that would challenge Rome for dominance of the known world, reshape the military thinking of the Arab world, and leave its fingerprints on the armored knights of medieval Europe.

Understanding the Sasanian military means understanding not just how they fought, but why they fought that way - what social structures produced their armies, what strategic pressures shaped their tactics, and where, ultimately, the cracks in that formidable machine began to show.

Elite Cavalry and Tactics

The backbone of Sasanian military power was its heavy cavalry, and no figure did more to define that arm than **Shapur II**, who ruled from 309 to 379 AD. Faced with the increasingly disciplined and well-equipped legions of Rome, Shapur recognized that conventional cavalry - fast, lightly armored, reliant on harassment and archery - was no longer enough. Rome had adapted. Persia needed to adapt faster.

His answer was the *savaran*: the noble horseman, drawn from the Persian aristocracy and equipped with armor that covered not just the rider but the horse itself. Lamellar plates of iron or hardened leather protected the mount's neck, flanks, and chest. The rider wore a full coat of mail, a visored helmet, and carried a heavy lance - the *kontos* - long enough to unseat an opponent before he could close to sword range. This was not a skirmisher. This was a human battering ram.

Shapur refined this concept into what historians sometimes call the super-heavy cavalry, a force designed specifically to break Roman formations through sheer momentum and mass. Where Roman infantry relied on disciplined close-quarters fighting, the Sasanian heavy cavalryman aimed to shatter that discipline before it could be brought to bear - to hit the line so hard, so fast, and with such concentrated force that it simply ceased to exist as a coherent unit.

But the Sasanians were never a one-trick army. Alongside the armored *savaran* rode lighter cavalry - faster, more mobile, expert with the composite bow. These horsemen could harry an enemy's flanks, cut off retreating units, and draw opposing formations out of position before the heavy cavalry delivered the killing blow. The combination was deliberate and sophisticated: fix the enemy with archery, disrupt their cohesion, then crash through with iron.

Infantry played a supporting role rather than a starring one. Sasanian foot soldiers - often drawn from lower social classes or subject peoples - held ground, protected supply lines, and guarded siege operations. They were competent, but they were not the point. In the Sasanian military imagination, battles were won on horseback.

Archers, too, were integral. Persian archery had been legendary since the days of Achaemenid Persia, and the Sasanians maintained that tradition. Horse archers in particular gave Sasanian commanders a flexibility that purely heavy cavalry forces lacked - the ability to engage at range, to probe enemy positions, and to retreat without committing to a decisive engagement until the moment was right.

The tactical result was an army that could fight in multiple registers: it could besiege, it could skirmish, it could deliver a devastating shock assault. Few armies of the ancient world matched that range.

Military Organization

Behind the battlefield brilliance lay a carefully structured institution. Sasanian military organization was inseparable from the empire's social hierarchy - a fact that gave it both its greatest strengths and, eventually, its most dangerous weaknesses.

At the apex stood the *shahanshah* - the King of Kings - who was in theory the supreme commander of all Sasanian forces. In practice, day-to-day command fell to a senior military official, the *eran-spahbod*, who oversaw operations across the empire's vast territories. Below him, regional commanders managed the defense of specific frontiers and provinces, creating a layered command structure that could respond to threats on multiple fronts simultaneously.

The cavalry itself was drawn overwhelmingly from the *azatan* - the Persian nobility. Military service was not merely a duty for these men; it was the foundation of their social identity and their claim to land and privilege. A noble who could not fight, who could not afford to equip himself and his horse for war, risked losing his standing entirely. This created a powerful incentive for military excellence, but it also meant that the quality of the cavalry was directly tied to the health of the aristocracy.

Equipping a *savaran* warrior was enormously expensive. The armor alone - for both rider and horse - represented a significant investment of iron, leather, and skilled labor. Add the horse itself, weapons, and the logistical support required to keep a heavily armored cavalryman in the field, and the cost becomes staggering. Only a prosperous noble class could sustain such a force, and only a prosperous empire could sustain such a noble class.

Supporting the cavalry were units of war elephants, acquired largely through trade and tribute from India. Elephants served primarily as psychological weapons and mobile platforms - their sheer size and noise could break the nerve of infantry and cavalry horses alike. They were not decisive on their own, but deployed at the right moment, they could tip a battle.

Logistics and supply were managed through a system of royal storehouses and requisition from subject territories. The empire's road network - inherited in part from earlier Persian dynasties - allowed for the relatively rapid movement of troops and supplies across the Iranian plateau, though the sheer scale of the empire always made sustained campaigning a logistical challenge.

Fortifications and Borders

An empire that spent four centuries at war with Rome to the west and nomadic peoples to the north and east could not rely on offensive power alone. The Sasanians invested heavily in fixed defenses, and the results were among the most impressive military engineering projects of the ancient world.

The western frontier - the long, contested borderland with Rome and later Byzantium - was defended through a combination of fortified cities, garrison towns, and natural barriers. Nisibis, Dara, and

Ctesiphon itself served as anchors of the western defense, cities capable of withstanding prolonged siege and serving as bases for offensive operations.

To the north, the threat came from the steppe: Hunnic confederacies, later Turkic peoples, and a shifting cast of nomadic powers that periodically swept down from Central Asia. Here the Sasanians built something remarkable - a series of long walls and fortified lines stretching across the Gorgan plain in northeastern Iran. The Gorgan Wall, sometimes called the "Great Wall of Iran," ran for roughly 200 kilometers and was defended by a series of forts spaced along its length. In scale and ambition, it was comparable to Hadrian's Wall in Britain - and it served a similar purpose: not to make invasion impossible, but to slow it, channel it, and give defenders time to respond.

These fortifications reflected a strategic reality that pure offensive power could not address. The Sasanian army was formidable in open battle, but it could not be everywhere at once. Walls and forts extended the reach of a finite military force, allowing smaller garrisons to hold ground while the main army concentrated elsewhere.

Reforms Over Time

No military institution survives four centuries unchanged, and the Sasanian war machine was no exception. As the empire's strategic environment shifted, so did its armies.

The reign of **Khosrow II**, who came to power in 590 or 591 AD, represents both the peak of Sasanian military ambition and the beginning of its unraveling. Khosrow launched the most aggressive campaigns in Sasanian history, pushing deep into Byzantine territory and, for a brief moment in the early 7th century, controlling Egypt, Syria, and much of Anatolia. His armies reached the walls of Constantinople. It seemed, for a few extraordinary years, that Persia might finally extinguish its ancient rival.

To sustain these campaigns, Khosrow expanded and reorganized the military, drawing on new sources of manpower and experimenting with combined-arms tactics on a larger scale than his predecessors. The army that fought under his banner was, in many respects, the most powerful Sasanian force ever assembled.

But the very success of those campaigns created the conditions for catastrophe. The wars exhausted the treasury, depopulated frontier regions, and strained the loyalty of the nobility. When the Byzantine emperor Heraclius launched his stunning counter-offensive in the 620s - striking deep into Persian territory while Sasanian forces were overextended - the empire had little resilience left. Khosrow was overthrown and killed by his own nobles in 628. In the decade that followed, the empire cycled through more than a dozen rulers, each weaker than the last.

By the time the Arab armies arrived in force in the 630s and 640s, the Sasanian military - still formidable on paper - was fighting with a fraction of its former cohesion and resources.

Strengths and Vulnerabilities

What made the Sasanian war machine so effective for so long was the same thing that made it brittle in the end: its deep entanglement with the social order that produced it.

As long as the Persian nobility was prosperous, loyal, and motivated, the *savaran* cavalry was nearly unmatched in the ancient world. Its influence spread far beyond Persia's borders - Roman commanders adopted elements of heavy cavalry tactics after encountering the Sasanians, and the Arab warriors who eventually conquered the empire carried Sasanian military traditions into their own expanding world. Scholars trace lines of influence from the Sasanian *savaran* to the armored horsemen of medieval Anatolia and, ultimately, to the knights of medieval Europe.

But a military built on aristocratic service was vulnerable to aristocratic politics. When the nobility fractured - when regional lords pursued their own interests over the empire's, when succession crises paralyzed central command - the war machine lost the coordination that made it deadly. Heavy cavalry requires logistics, training, and unified command. Without those, even the finest armored horseman is just an expensive target.

The Arab conquests of the 630s and 640s did not simply overpower the Sasanian military. They exploited a system already weakened by decades of overextension, civil war, and institutional decay. The iron wall, it turned out, had been rusting from within.

Quick Summary

- The **Sasanian Empire** (AD 224-642) was the last great Persian empire before the Arab conquests and Rome's most persistent rival in the classical world.

- **Shapur II** developed the super-heavy *savaran* cavalry - fully armored riders on armored horses - specifically to counter Roman military strength.

- Sasanian tactics combined heavy shock cavalry, light horse archers, infantry, and war elephants into a flexible combined-arms force.

- Military organization was tied to the Persian nobility, whose social status depended on military service, creating high-quality but socially fragile forces.

- Fortifications like the Gorgan Wall extended Sasanian defensive reach along vulnerable northern frontiers, complementing offensive cavalry power.

- **Khosrow II's** early 7th-century campaigns represented the peak of Sasanian military ambition - and triggered the overextension that accelerated the empire's collapse.

- Sasanian military traditions influenced Roman, Arab, Turkish, and medieval European warfare, making this one of the most consequential military cultures of the ancient world.

The Sasanian war machine did not simply disappear when the last king fell. It dissolved into the armies that defeated it, its tactics and technologies absorbed by the very forces that had overwhelmed it. The Arab warriors who swept across Persia in the 640s rode, in many ways, in the shadow of the empire they had conquered - and passed that shadow forward into the medieval world. What the Sasanians built in iron and discipline outlasted the empire itself, echoing across centuries in the armor of knights and the tactics of horsemen who had never heard the name of Shapur II.

Chapter 13:
A World of Rivals and Allies - Sasanian Diplomacy

When Khusrow II sent an embassy to the Byzantine emperor Maurice in the late sixth century, the gifts that traveled with it were extraordinary: bolts of silk, exotic animals, finely worked silver vessels, and letters composed in the elevated language of royal equals. This was not generosity. It was strategy. Every object carried a message about power, civilization, and the terms on which two empires might coexist - or not.

The Sasanians did not only make war. They made relationships.

For more than four centuries, from the rise of Ardashir I in 224 AD to the empire's collapse in 651 AD, the Sasanian Empire - known in its own sources as *Eranshahr*, the realm of the Iranians - sat at the crossroads of the ancient world. To the west lay Rome, then Byzantium. To the north and east stretched the vast Eurasian steppe and the kingdoms of Central Asia. To the south, the Arabian Peninsula simmered with tribal politics. And beyond the horizons, India and China glittered as trading partners and diplomatic counterparts. Managing all of these relationships simultaneously required something more than military force. It required a sophisticated, deliberate, and often ruthless foreign policy.

Sasanian diplomacy was not a footnote to Sasanian warfare. It was its equal partner. Marriages sealed alliances. Gifts communicated hierarchy. Refugees became leverage. Tribal leaders on distant frontiers received Sasanian silver and Sasanian recognition - and in return, they guarded borders that no standing army could fully cover. What follows traces the Sasanian Empire outward from its Iranian heartland, mapping the web of relationships it built, maintained, and sometimes deliberately broke across the known world.

Relations with Central Asia and the Steppe

The northeastern frontier of the Sasanian Empire was never quiet. Beyond the great mountain ranges and river valleys of eastern Iran lay the steppe - a vast, rolling corridor of grassland stretching from the Caspian Sea deep into Central Asia, home to nomadic confederacies of extraordinary military power. For the Sasanians, this frontier was both a threat and an opportunity, and managing it demanded constant diplomatic attention.

The most formidable of these steppe powers were the Huns and, later, the Hephthalites - a confederation known to the Sasanians as the *Hayatila* - who dominated Central Asia from roughly the late fourth century onward. At their height, the Hephthalites were capable of inflicting catastrophic defeats on Sasanian armies. In 484 AD, the Sasanian king Peroz I led a campaign against them and was killed in battle, along with much of his army. It was one of the most devastating military disasters in Sasanian history, and it forced the empire into a period of tribute payments to its northeastern neighbors.

But the relationship was never simply one of dominance and submission. When circumstances shifted, the Sasanians proved adept at turning former enemies into useful partners. In the late sixth century, Khusrow I forged a strategic alliance with a new steppe power - the Western Türks - and together they crushed the Hephthalite confederation around 557 AD. This was Sasanian diplomacy at its most calculated: using one rival to destroy another, then managing the new power that emerged.

Central Asia also mattered economically. The Silk Road, that great network of overland trade routes connecting China to the Mediterranean, passed directly through Sasanian-controlled and Sasanian-adjacent territory. Control over, or at least favorable access to, these routes was a persistent Sasanian strategic interest. Sogdian merchants - the great middlemen of the ancient Silk Road, based in the cities of Samarkand and Bukhara - operated within a diplomatic and commercial environment that the Sasanians worked hard to shape. Sasanian silver coins, found in hoards across Central Asia and as far as China, are a material reminder of how deeply the empire's commercial reach extended into this world.

The steppe frontier also produced a steady stream of refugees, defectors, and political exiles - and the Sasanians learned to use them. A displaced chieftain offered asylum at the Sasanian court became a tool of pressure against his homeland. A Hephthalite prince sheltered in Ctesiphon was a potential future client king. Hospitality, in Sasanian diplomacy, was rarely purely generous. It was almost always useful.

Arabia and Tribal Politics

South of the Sasanian heartland lay a different kind of frontier - not a wall of mountains or a river boundary, but a vast, porous desert. Arabia was not an empty space in Sasanian strategic thinking. It was a zone of tribal politics, caravan routes, and competing loyalties that required constant management.

The Sasanians approached Arabia primarily through client relationships with Arab tribal confederacies. The most important of these was the Lakhmid kingdom, centered at the city of al-Hira in what is now southern Iraq. For generations, the Lakhmids served as a Sasanian buffer state - a semi-autonomous Arab kingdom that guarded the desert frontier, conducted raids against Byzantine-aligned Arab tribes, and provided the Sasanians with intelligence, military auxiliaries, and a degree of political influence deep into the Arabian Peninsula.

The relationship was mutually beneficial, but also hierarchical. Lakhmid kings received Sasanian recognition, gifts, and occasionally military support. In return, they remained within the Sasanian orbit and performed the difficult, unglamorous work of frontier management that no Sasanian army could do as effectively. Al-Hira itself became a notable center of Arab culture and poetry, a place where Iranian and Arab worlds intersected in ways that would have lasting cultural consequences.

Yet the Sasanians also demonstrated the limits of client-state diplomacy when they abolished the Lakhmid kingdom entirely in 602 AD, executing the last Lakhmid king, al-Nu'man III, and incorporating the region under direct Sasanian administration. The reasons remain debated, but the consequences were severe. Without the Lakhmids as a buffer, the Arabian frontier became dangerously exposed. Some historians have argued that this decision, made under Khusrow II, contributed directly to the vulnerability that allowed the early Islamic armies to advance so rapidly into Sasanian territory just decades later.

Arabia also brought the Sasanians into indirect competition with Byzantium for influence over Yemen - the wealthy southwestern corner of the Arabian Peninsula, home to the ancient Himyarite kingdom and a critical node in the Indian Ocean trade network. In the sixth century, both empires backed rival factions in a series of Yemeni political struggles, with the Sasanians eventually establishing a presence there around 570 AD. Control of Yemen meant influence over the sea lanes connecting the Persian Gulf to East Africa and India - a prize worth considerable diplomatic and military investment.

India, China, and the Edges of the World

If the steppe and Arabia represented the Sasanian Empire's most urgent diplomatic challenges, India and China represented something different: the outer edges of a connected world in which Persia occupied a central, privileged position.

Sasanian relations with the Indian subcontinent were shaped primarily by trade and cultural exchange rather than territorial ambition. The Persian Gulf was a Sasanian-dominated waterway, and the port cities along its shores - including the great emporium of Siraf - served as hubs for maritime commerce connecting the Iranian plateau to the Malabar Coast, Sri Lanka, and beyond. Indian spices, textiles, and precious stones flowed westward through Sasanian-controlled waters; Sasanian silver and manufactured goods moved east in return.

Diplomatic contacts with Indian kingdoms were real, if less formally documented than Sasanian relations with Rome or Byzantium. Sasanian art shows clear Indian influences, particularly in textile patterns and certain decorative motifs, suggesting sustained cultural contact. Indian scholars and physicians are recorded at the Sasanian court, most notably during the reign of Khusrow I, when the royal court at Ctesiphon became a gathering point for intellectuals from across the known world. The game of chess - originating in India - reportedly reached the Sasanian court during this period, a small but telling marker of the intellectual traffic moving along these routes.

China represented the far end of the Silk Road, and the relationship between the Sasanian Empire and the various Chinese dynasties was conducted primarily through trade and formal embassy. Chinese sources record multiple Sasanian embassies arriving at the courts of the Han, Wei, and later Tang dynasties, bearing gifts and seeking commercial relationships. Sasanian merchants and their Sogdian intermediaries carried Persian goods - glassware, silver, textiles - deep into Chinese territory, and Chinese silks and ceramics made the return journey westward.

When the Sasanian Empire fell to the Arab conquests in 651 AD, the last Sasanian prince, Peroz III, fled eastward and eventually sought refuge at the Tang court in China. The Tang emperor received him, granted him a title, and gave him a small military escort, though the attempt to reclaim the Sasanian throne came to nothing. That a Persian prince could travel to China and find a court that knew who he was speaks to the depth of the connections the Sasanian Empire had built across the continent.

The Art of Diplomacy: Gifts, Marriages, and Treaties

Sasanian diplomacy operated through a sophisticated vocabulary of symbolic exchange that its neighbors understood and respected - and that the Sasanians deployed with considerable skill.

Gifts were the primary language of inter-imperial communication. Silk, the most prestigious commodity of the ancient world, moved constantly between courts as a marker of status and goodwill. Sasanian kings sent bolts of royal silk, silver vessels decorated with hunting scenes, and exotic animals - lions, elephants, rare birds - to Byzantine emperors, Chinese courts, and steppe chieftains alike. These were not merely generous gestures. Each gift carried an implicit message about the giver's wealth, sophistication, and power. To receive a Sasanian gift was to acknowledge, at least implicitly, a relationship on Sasanian terms.

Marriage alliances were another instrument of statecraft. Royal women were dispatched to seal agreements with neighboring powers, and foreign princesses were received into the Sasanian harem as living symbols of diplomatic relationships. These arrangements bound ruling families together across generations and created personal stakes in the maintenance of peaceful relations - though they could also become sources of tension when political circumstances changed.

Treaties between the Sasanians and Byzantium were among the most formally elaborate diplomatic instruments of the ancient world. They specified border arrangements, the treatment of merchants and travelers, the status of religious minorities, and the payment of subsidies - the Byzantines often paid the Sasanians substantial sums in exchange for Sasanian management of the Caucasian passes through which steppe raiders might otherwise pour. These payments were diplomatically framed as contributions to a shared defensive burden, not as tribute, a distinction that mattered enormously to Byzantine pride.

The Sasanian court itself served as a stage for diplomatic theater. Foreign ambassadors were received with elaborate ceremony, made to wait in carefully calibrated ways, and granted audiences designed to communicate the king's cosmic authority. The physical setting - the great audience hall at Ctesiphon, with its famous vaulted arch - was itself a diplomatic instrument, a built argument for Sasanian greatness.

Persia's Place in a Connected World

Stepping back from individual relationships, what emerges is a portrait of an empire that understood itself as the center of a connected world - and worked systematically to maintain that position.

The Sasanians occupied a genuinely privileged geographic location. Every major trade route between the Mediterranean and East Asia passed through or adjacent to their territory. Every significant power of the era - Rome, Byzantium, the steppe confederacies, the kingdoms of India and Arabia, the dynasties of China - had reasons to maintain relationships with Ctesiphon. The Sasanians leveraged this centrality with considerable sophistication, playing rivals against each other, controlling access to trade routes, and projecting an image of imperial grandeur that commanded respect even from enemies.

This connected position also shaped Sasanian culture in profound ways. The court at Ctesiphon absorbed Greek philosophy, Indian mathematics, Syriac Christian theology, and Central Asian artistic traditions. Sasanian silver plates, with their scenes of royal hunts and feasts, were collected and imitated from the steppes of Russia to the courts of Tang China. Sasanian architectural forms influenced

Byzantine churches and Central Asian palaces. The empire was not merely a node in a network. It was a cultural transmitter, taking in influences from across the known world and sending transformed versions outward again.

When the Sasanian Empire fell, the world it had helped to organize did not simply disappear. The Islamic caliphates that succeeded it inherited Sasanian administrative structures, diplomatic protocols, and cultural forms. Persian remained a language of high culture and statecraft across a vast swath of the post-conquest world. The memory of *Eranshahr* - the realm of the Iranians - persisted as an ideal and an identity long after the last Sasanian king had died.

Quick Summary

- The Sasanian Empire (224-651 AD) maintained complex diplomatic relationships with powers across Eurasia, from Byzantium to China.

- On the northeastern frontier, the Sasanians managed shifting alliances with steppe powers including the Hephthalites and the Western Türks, using one to destroy the other when strategically advantageous.

- In Arabia, the Lakhmid kingdom served as a crucial Sasanian client state for generations; its abolition in 602 AD left the southern frontier dangerously exposed.

- Trade with India and China flowed primarily through the Persian Gulf and the Silk Road, with Sasanian silver coins and luxury goods reaching as far as East Asia.

- Diplomatic tools included elaborate gift exchange, royal marriage alliances, and formally negotiated treaties - each carrying precise symbolic and political weight.

- The Sasanian court was a center of cultural synthesis, absorbing influences from Greek, Indian, Syriac, and Central Asian traditions and transmitting them outward.

- After the empire's fall, Sasanian administrative and cultural forms survived within the Islamic caliphates, ensuring that Sasanian diplomatic and political legacies outlasted the empire itself.

Four centuries of sustained engagement with the wider world left marks that outlasted the empire by centuries. The Sasanians grasped something that purely military powers rarely do: dominance maintained only by force is always temporary, but dominance woven into trade, culture, and mutual interest can persist long after the armies have gone home. Their world was one of rivals and allies, of calculated gifts and careful marriages, of silver coins traveling roads that crossed half the known world. That world ended in 651 AD. The connections it built did not.

Part 5
Culture and Civilization

Chapter 14:
Wealth of an Empire

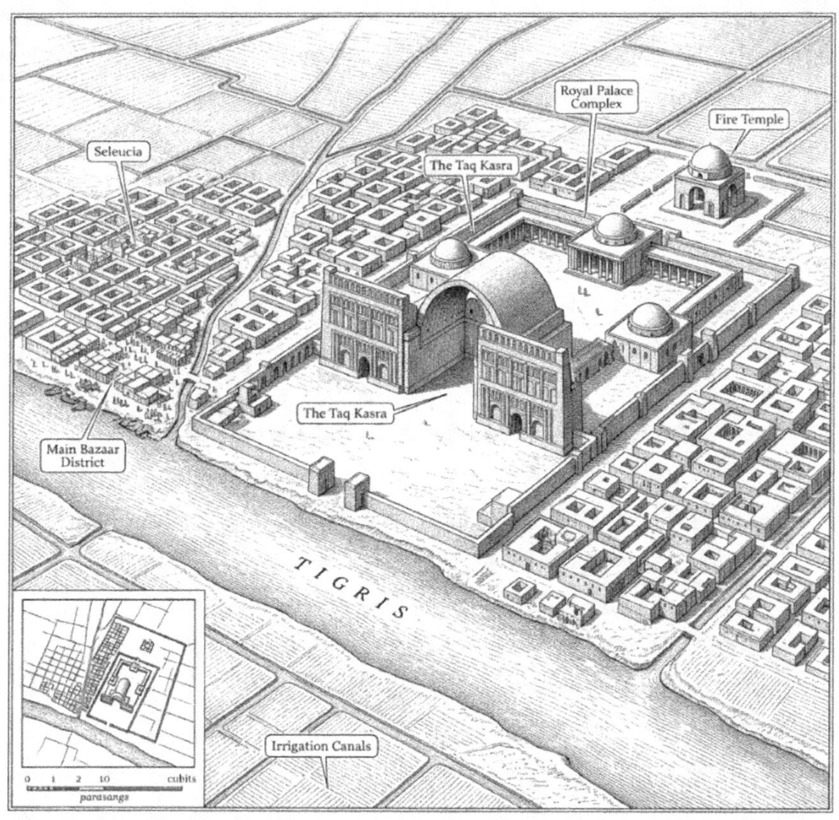

Ctesiphon: Reconstruction of the Sasanian Capital

Power flowed not just from armies - but from wealth. Rome's legions could conquer territory, but it was grain, gold, and commerce that held an empire together.

The Engine Beneath the Eagle

When we think of Rome at its height, we tend to picture marble columns, gladiatorial combat, or the disciplined march of legions across foreign soil. What we picture less often is the farmer knee-deep in an irrigation ditch, the merchant haggling over silk at a dusty crossroads market, or the tax collector tallying grain receipts in a provincial town. Yet these figures - unglamorous, largely nameless - were the true foundation of Roman power.

An empire is, at its core, an economic enterprise. Conquest brings territory, but territory must be administered, fed, defended, and taxed. Rome understood this with a clarity that few ancient states could match. From the first century BCE through the fifth century CE, the Roman Empire built and maintained one of the ancient world's most sophisticated economic systems - one that drew on the agricultural productivity of its vast heartland, the long-distance commerce of the Silk Road, and a state apparatus capable of extracting and redistributing enormous quantities of wealth.

That system was neither perfectly efficient nor uniformly prosperous. Wealth disparities ran deep. Nutritional deficiencies existed alongside plenty. Structural vulnerabilities accumulated beneath the surface of imperial confidence. But for centuries, the Roman economy generated enough surplus to fund armies, build infrastructure, sustain cities, and project power across three continents.

What follows traces how Rome built that economic engine - and where, quietly, its cracks began to show.

Agriculture, Irrigation, and the Productive Heartland

Every great ancient civilization rested on agriculture, and Rome was no exception. The empire's economic foundation was the soil - the wheat fields of North Africa, the olive groves of Spain, the vineyards of Gaul, the grain-producing flatlands of Egypt. These were not merely sources of food. They were engines of surplus, and surplus was the precondition for everything else Rome wanted to do.

Egypt deserves particular attention. When Rome absorbed it following the death of Cleopatra in 30 BCE, it acquired what was effectively the ancient world's most productive breadbasket. The Nile's annual floods deposited rich silt across the floodplain, enabling yields that other regions could not approach. Roman administrators recognized this immediately and treated Egypt as a special imperial possession - too valuable to be governed by a senator who might develop his own power base there. Instead, Egypt was administered directly by a prefect answering to the emperor alone.

The evidence from Roman Egypt paints a complex picture. Much of the population appears to have been relatively healthy and economically functional by ancient standards. Yet nutritional deficiencies were present in parts of the population, a reminder that agricultural abundance did not distribute itself evenly. The peasant farmer who worked the land rarely captured much of the value he produced. Rents, taxes, and obligations to landlords consumed a significant portion of agricultural output before it ever reached the farmer's own table.

Irrigation was central to this productive capacity. Across the empire - from the arid stretches of North Africa to the river valleys of the Near East - Roman engineers and local populations maintained and expanded irrigation networks that transformed marginal land into productive farmland. These were not always Roman innovations; many systems predated Roman rule by centuries. But Rome's administrative capacity helped maintain and sometimes extend them, ensuring that agricultural output remained high enough to feed cities, supply armies, and generate taxable surplus.

Land ownership itself was a marker of status and a source of economic mobility - but only for some. Evidence suggests that certain peasants did manage to improve their economic standing by acquiring land over time, working their way into a more secure position. This was the exception, not the rule. For the majority, agricultural life meant subsistence-level existence within a system that extracted heavily from those at the bottom.

What Rome's agricultural economy did brilliantly was concentrate that extracted surplus and redirect it. Grain from Egypt and North Africa fed the city of Rome itself - a metropolis of perhaps a million people who could not possibly feed themselves from the surrounding Italian countryside alone. The logistics of moving that grain - by ship across the Mediterranean, then upriver, then by cart - required infrastructure, organization, and investment on a scale that no private enterprise could have managed. The state made it work, and in doing so, made Rome possible.

The Silk Road: Trade Routes and Revenue

Rome did not build the Silk Road. No single empire did. What the Silk Road represented was something more organic and more remarkable: a web of overlapping trade networks stretching from the Mediterranean coast to the markets of Central Asia and China, connecting civilizations that had only the haziest awareness of each other's existence.

Rome entered this web as both a consumer and, to a lesser extent, a supplier. The goods that flowed westward along these routes - silk, spices, precious stones, exotic animals, glassware - found eager buyers among Rome's wealthy classes. Silk, in particular, became a cultural phenomenon. Lightweight, lustrous, and extraordinarily expensive, it became a symbol of status and refinement among Rome's elite. Roman writers occasionally complained about the drain of gold that silk imports represented, suggesting that the trade balance was not always comfortable for Rome's treasury.

But the Silk Road was never just a road, and it was never just about silk. It was a system of relay trade in which goods passed through many hands across enormous distances, each exchange adding value and cost. Roman merchants rarely traveled to China, and Chinese merchants rarely reached Rome. Instead, goods moved through a chain of intermediaries - Parthian, Sogdian, Indian, and Arabian traders who each took their cut and who each possessed knowledge of their particular segment of the route that gave them genuine commercial power.

Rome's engagement with this system shaped its economy and its culture in ways that went beyond mere commerce. Eastern technologies and philosophical traditions filtered westward along the same routes that carried silk and spices. The Silk Road was, in this sense, a transmission belt for ideas as well as goods, and Rome absorbed both.

For the imperial state, long-distance trade represented both opportunity and challenge. Customs duties collected at ports and border crossings contributed meaningfully to imperial revenues. Infrastructure investment along key routes, including roads and way stations, helped facilitate commerce and, by extension, the tax revenues it generated. Empires that understood this dynamic invested in connectivity; those that did not found themselves cut off from the prosperity that trade could generate.

Rome understood it. The empire's road network - legendary for its engineering quality and geographic reach - was built primarily for military movement, but it served commerce equally well. A road that could move a legion could move a merchant's wagon. The same infrastructure that projected military power also projected economic integration, binding the empire's diverse regions into something approaching a single market.

Merchants, Markets, and the Flow of Goods

Within the empire's borders, commerce moved through a dense network of local and regional markets. Roman cities were commercial centers as much as administrative ones. The forum - that central public space at the heart of every Roman city - was not only a place for civic life and political display; it was where business got done.

Merchants occupied a complicated position in Roman society. Roman aristocratic ideology officially disdained trade as beneath the dignity of a gentleman, who was supposed to derive his income from land. In practice, wealthy Romans participated in commerce through intermediaries, investing in trading ventures while maintaining the fiction of agricultural respectability. The actual work of buying and selling fell to a class of professional merchants - some free, some freedmen, some operating as agents for wealthy patrons - who moved goods across the empire with impressive efficiency.

What moved through these markets? Almost everything. Grain and olive oil traveled in enormous quantities, the staple commodities of Mediterranean life. Wine moved in amphorae from producing regions to consuming ones. Pottery, metalwork, textiles, timber, and building materials all circulated through networks of trade that connected the empire's diverse productive regions. A pot made in a workshop in Gaul might end up on a table in Roman Britain. Spanish olive oil might lubricate a lamp in Roman Egypt.

This internal trade was not merely a luxury - it was structurally necessary. Rome's cities, including Rome itself, could not sustain their populations without continuous imports of food and goods from the surrounding countryside and from more distant provinces. The empire's urban population depended on the smooth functioning of commercial networks in a way that would have been immediately recognizable to anyone living in a modern city.

Wealth disparities shaped who benefited from this commerce. Evidence points clearly to significant gaps between the wealthy elite and the broader population. Some individuals accumulated fortunes through trade, land, and imperial favor. Others lived at or near subsistence level, vulnerable to harvest failures, price spikes, and the ordinary misfortunes of ancient life. The Roman economy was not a rising tide that lifted all boats equally.

Taxation, Coinage, and State Finance

None of Rome's economic achievements - the roads, the grain supply, the armies, the administration - came free. They required revenue, and revenue required a system of extraction that could reach into every corner of an empire spanning millions of square kilometers.

Rome's tax system was extensive, if not always efficient by modern standards. Land taxes formed the backbone of imperial revenue, assessed on the productive capacity of agricultural land across the provinces. Customs duties collected at ports and provincial borders added another stream of income. Inheritance taxes, poll taxes in certain provinces, and levies on specific transactions all contributed to the imperial treasury.

Coinage was the lubricant that made this system function. Rome maintained a currency system based on gold, silver, and bronze coins, and the ability to pay taxes in coin - rather than in kind - was both a convenience and a mechanism of economic integration. To pay taxes in Roman coin, provincial populations had to participate in the Roman monetary economy, which meant selling goods or labor for coin, which meant engaging with markets, which meant deeper integration into the imperial economic system. It was a self-reinforcing cycle that bound the provinces to Rome in ways that went beyond mere political submission.

The state also spent heavily, and its spending patterns shaped the economy in significant ways. Military pay was one of the largest expenditure items, and soldiers - stationed across the empire - spent their wages locally, stimulating economic activity in frontier regions that might otherwise have been economically marginal. Public building programs, grain subsidies for Rome's urban population, and the maintenance of roads and harbors all represented forms of state investment that had economic multiplier effects.

Economic Strengths and Structural Weaknesses

Rome's economy had genuine strengths. Its geographic scale created opportunities for specialization and exchange that smaller political units could not match. Its infrastructure - roads, ports, aqueducts - reduced the costs of moving goods and people. Its legal system provided a framework for contracts and property rights that gave merchants and investors a degree of security. Its currency system facilitated trade across enormous distances.

But structural weaknesses ran alongside these strengths, and they mattered.

Wealth concentration was one. The gap between Rome's wealthy elite and its broader population was substantial. While some peasants managed to improve their position by acquiring land, the majority of the agricultural population lived in conditions of significant economic precarity. Relative poverty was a persistent feature of Roman life, even if the evidence does not suggest a steady worsening of absolute poverty across the empire's history.

Nutritional deficiencies documented in parts of the population - including in the relatively prosperous province of Egypt - point to the limits of agricultural abundance when distribution is unequal. Food was produced in large quantities, but it did not always reach those who needed it most.

The economy also remained fundamentally dependent on agricultural output in a way that made it vulnerable to climatic variation, harvest failures, and the disruptions that came with political instability. When the political system faltered - as it did with increasing frequency from the third century CE onward - the economic consequences were severe. Trade networks contracted, coinage was debased, and the integrated market that Rome had built began to fragment.

These were not fatal flaws in themselves. Every economic system has structural vulnerabilities. What matters is whether the system can adapt and absorb shocks - and for centuries, Rome's did. The cracks, when they finally widened into fractures, did so slowly, and the story of how they did belongs to later chapters.

Quick Summary

- Rome's economy rested on agricultural surplus, with Egypt serving as the empire's most productive and strategically vital breadbasket.

- Irrigation networks, maintained and sometimes expanded under Roman administration, sustained agricultural output across diverse regions.

- The Silk Road connected Rome to a vast web of long-distance trade, bringing silk, spices, and cultural influences westward while generating customs revenues for the imperial state.

- Internal trade moved goods - grain, oil, wine, pottery, metalwork - across the empire through dense networks of markets and merchants, binding diverse provinces into an integrated economic system.

- Rome's tax system, built around land taxes and customs duties, extracted surplus from across the empire and funded armies, infrastructure, and urban food supplies.

- Coinage served as both a commercial tool and a mechanism of economic integration, drawing provincial populations into the Roman monetary economy.

- Wealth disparities were significant and persistent: some individuals prospered and even rose economically, but the majority of the agricultural population lived in conditions of precarity.

- Structural vulnerabilities - wealth concentration, dependence on agricultural output, susceptibility to political disruption - coexisted with genuine economic strengths for centuries before eventually contributing to the empire's long decline.

Rome's economic achievement was real, and it was remarkable. For roughly five centuries, the empire sustained a level of economic integration, commercial activity, and material prosperity that the

Western world would not see again for more than a thousand years. That achievement rested on the labor of millions of farmers, the enterprise of thousands of merchants, and the organizational capacity of a state that understood, better than most, that power without wealth is temporary - and wealth without systems is fleeting.

Chapter 15:
Cities of Power

A city is never just buildings. It is a declaration.

When Ardashir I founded the city of Gōr in the early third century CE, he wasn't simply constructing a capital - he was announcing to the world that a new empire had arrived, one with the ambition, the resources, and the organizational will to reshape the landscape itself. Cities were how the Sasanian Empire made itself legible: to its subjects, to its rivals, and to the merchants and diplomats who traveled its roads from China to the Mediterranean. They were the nodes through which power flowed, where taxes were collected, where armies were provisioned, where cultures collided and commerce flourished.

The Sasanian Empire - known in its own sources as *Eranshahr*, the realm of the Iranians - lasted from 224 CE to 651 CE, and for more than four centuries it ranked among the most formidable states on earth. At its height, it stretched from Mesopotamia in the west to the edges of Central Asia in the east, encompassing a staggering diversity of peoples, languages, and landscapes. Holding all of this together required more than military force. It required cities.

What follows traces the urban spine of the Sasanian world - from the great imperial capital at Ctesiphon to the planned foundations of early Sasanian kings, from the administrative machinery housed within city walls to the merchants, artisans, and ordinary residents who gave those cities their pulse. What emerges is a portrait of an empire that understood, perhaps better than any of its contemporaries, that civilization is built in stone and brick, one city at a time.

Ctesiphon: Heart of the Empire

No city in the Sasanian world carried more weight than Ctesiphon.

Situated on the eastern bank of the Tigris River in what is now central Iraq, Ctesiphon had been a place of consequence long before the Sasanians came to power. Its origins stretched back to the Parthian era, when Mithridates I - who ruled from roughly 171 to 132 BCE - established it as a royal encampment near the older Hellenistic city of Seleucia. Over the following centuries, the two cities grew into one another, forming a vast urban agglomeration that contemporaries sometimes called "the twin cities." Together, they commanded the most strategically valuable stretch of the Tigris, sitting at the crossroads of trade routes that connected the Persian Gulf to the Mediterranean world.

Vologases I, who reigned from roughly 51 to 80 CE, accelerated Ctesiphon's rise by actively encouraging trade and expanding the city's reach. By the time the Sasanians seized power in 224 CE, Ctesiphon was already one of the largest and most prosperous cities in the ancient world. Ardashir I and his successors did not abandon it. They inherited it, amplified it, and made it the beating heart of their empire.

As the Sasanian capital, Ctesiphon performed multiple roles simultaneously. It was the seat of the king of kings, the *shahanshah*, whose palace dominated the city's skyline. It was the administrative nerve center through which imperial decrees radiated outward to the provinces. It was a religious hub, home to Zoroastrian fire temples and, in time, to Christian and Jewish communities as well. And it was a commercial powerhouse, a city where goods arriving from China - silk, spices, precious stones - crossed the Tigris and entered the vast network of Sasanian and Roman trade.

The physical scale of Ctesiphon matched its ambitions. Ancient sources describe a city of extraordinary size, with a population that may have numbered in the hundreds of thousands at its peak, though precise figures remain difficult to establish. What is beyond dispute is the grandeur of its architecture. The most celebrated structure was the *Taq Kasra*, the great vaulted audience hall of the Sasanian palace, whose massive brick arch - spanning roughly 25 meters and rising to a height of approximately 37 meters - remains one of the largest single-span brick arches ever constructed. Even in its current ruined state, it commands awe. In its day, it would have been overwhelming.

Ctesiphon's wealth rested on geography as much as governance. The Tigris was not merely a boundary; it was a highway. Merchants moved goods up and downstream, and the city's position allowed Sasanian authorities to tax, regulate, and profit from that flow. The proximity of Seleucia - and later the Sasanian foundation of Veh-Ardashir on the western bank - meant that the capital complex functioned almost as a city-state within the empire, dense with population, commerce, and institutional power.

Ctesiphon endured as a major urban center until 637 CE, when Arab Muslim forces defeated the Sasanian army at the Battle of al-Qadisiyyah and swept into the capital. Its fall marked the effective end of the Sasanian Empire. But for four centuries before that moment, it had stood as one of the great cities of the ancient world - a rival to Rome, to Constantinople, to Chang'an.

Urban Planning and Design

Ctesiphon was the empire's crown jewel, but it was not the only city that revealed Sasanian ambitions in brick and mortar.

When Ardashir I founded the city of Gōr - later known as Firuzabad - in the province of Fars in the early third century CE, he was doing something deliberate and ideologically charged. Gōr was a planned city, laid out according to a circular design that reflected both Zoroastrian cosmological principles and a very practical desire to project royal authority. The circular plan was not accidental. It announced order, symmetry, and centralized power - a city shaped like a mandala, with the palace and fire temple at its heart and the population arranged around them.

This kind of intentional urban design was a hallmark of early Sasanian city-building. Ardashir and his successors understood that cities were not simply functional necessities; they were statements. A well-planned city with wide avenues, imposing public buildings, and clear administrative zones communicated something about the nature of the regime that built it. It said: we are organized, we are powerful, and we intend to last.

Sasanian urban planning drew on a rich inheritance. The Achaemenid and Parthian empires had both left behind traditions of monumental architecture and city design, and Sasanian builders absorbed and adapted these influences while adding their own innovations. Fired brick, which had been used in Mesopotamia for millennia, remained a primary building material. But Sasanian architects also developed sophisticated techniques for constructing large vaulted spaces - the barrel vault, the dome on squinches - that would later pass into Islamic architecture and, through it, into the broader history of world building.

Cities were designed with defense in mind as well. Walls, gates, and moats were standard features of Sasanian urban foundations. Gōr's circular plan was reinforced by a defensive ditch and a ring wall, making the city as much a fortress as a residence. This combination of aesthetic ambition and military pragmatism ran through Sasanian urban design at every scale.

Water management was another critical dimension. In the arid and semi-arid landscapes of much of the empire, cities depended on sophisticated irrigation and canal systems to sustain their populations. Sasanian engineers extended and maintained networks of underground aqueducts known as *qanats*, as well as surface canals that fed both agricultural land and urban water supplies. A city without water was a city that could not grow - and the Sasanians, who wanted their cities to grow, invested accordingly.

Cities as Administrative Centers

Behind every Sasanian city's walls lay a machinery of governance that kept the empire running.

The Sasanian state was one of the most administratively sophisticated polities of the ancient world. It maintained a complex hierarchy of officials, from the great nobles and provincial governors at the top to local administrators and tax collectors at the base. Cities were the fixed points around which this hierarchy organized itself - where records were kept, courts convened, tribute was assessed and collected, and the king's representatives exercised authority over the surrounding countryside.

Provincial capitals served as the primary nodes of this administrative network. Each major region of the empire - Mesopotamia, Persia, Media, Khuzestan, and others - had its own urban center that functioned as a hub of royal power. These cities housed the residences of governors, the offices of scribes and accountants, the barracks of garrison troops, and the fire temples that gave Zoroastrian religious authority its physical presence. Administration and religion were not separate spheres in the Sasanian world; they reinforced each other, and cities were where that reinforcement was most visible.

The fiscal system depended entirely on urban infrastructure. Tax revenues from agriculture, trade, and craft production flowed into city treasuries before being forwarded to the central government. Markets were regulated, weights and measures were standardized, and commercial disputes were adjudicated by officials based in urban centers. Without cities, the Sasanian state could not have extracted the resources it needed to fund its armies, its building projects, or its court.

Cities also served as centers of record-keeping and legal administration. The Sasanian legal tradition, rooted in Zoroastrian law and elaborated over centuries of imperial practice, required literate officials capable of drafting contracts, recording land transactions, and adjudicating inheritance disputes. These officials were concentrated in cities, where the institutions that trained and employed them were located. The growth of Sasanian cities was inseparable from the growth of Sasanian bureaucracy - each fed the other.

Trade, Population, and Urban Growth

Commerce was the lifeblood of Sasanian cities, and the empire's geography made it one of history's great trading crossroads.

Sitting between the Roman and Byzantine worlds to the west and the Kushan and Chinese empires to the east, the Sasanian Empire occupied a position of extraordinary commercial advantage. The Silk Road - that loose network of overland and maritime routes connecting East Asia to the Mediterranean - passed through Sasanian territory, and the empire's rulers were determined to profit from it. Ctesiphon and Seleucia were among the primary beneficiaries, serving as transfer points where Chinese silk, Indian spices, and Central Asian gemstones changed hands before continuing westward.

This trade generated enormous wealth, and that wealth fed urban growth. Merchants needed warehouses, caravanserais, and markets. Artisans needed workshops and customers. Officials needed offices and residences. Religious institutions needed temples and endowments. All of these demands concentrated people and resources in cities, driving population growth and physical expansion.

Sasanian cities were ethnically and religiously diverse in ways that reflected the empire's commercial reach. Jewish communities, many descended from the populations deported to Mesopotamia during the Babylonian period, were well established in the cities of the western empire, particularly around Ctesiphon. Christian communities, including the Church of the East - sometimes called the Nestorian Church - had significant urban presences, especially after Christianity spread through the empire's trading networks. Zoroastrians formed the dominant religious community and the backbone of the imperial elite, but the cities of *Eranshahr* were far from religiously homogeneous.

Population figures for ancient cities are always approximate, but the scale of Sasanian urban centers was clearly substantial. Ctesiphon, at its height, was almost certainly among the most populous cities in the world. Smaller provincial capitals and market towns extended the urban network across the empire, creating a hierarchy of settlement that ranged from the imperial capital down to modest administrative towns serving local agricultural regions.

Urban Life and Culture

What was it actually like to live in a Sasanian city?

For the wealthy - the nobles, the high priests, the senior officials - city life meant access to luxury goods from across the known world, residence in palatial compounds, and participation in a courtly culture of considerable sophistication. Sasanian metalwork, textiles, and decorative arts were among the finest produced anywhere in the ancient world, and the cities were where these objects were made, displayed, and exchanged.

For the majority of urban residents - the artisans, merchants, laborers, and servants who made the cities function - life was harder but not without its own texture. Markets were social spaces as much as commercial ones. Religious festivals, centered on the fire temples and the Zoroastrian calendar, structured the rhythms of the year. Multiple religious communities living in proximity meant that urban neighborhoods often had a layered quality, with Jewish synagogues,

Christian churches, and Zoroastrian temples sometimes standing within walking distance of one another.

Cities were also places of intellectual life. The Sasanian period saw significant activity in medicine, astronomy, philosophy, and law, much of it concentrated in urban centers with the institutional infrastructure to support scholars. The great medical academy at Gundeshapur - one of the most celebrated centers of learning in the late antique world - was an urban institution, drawing physicians and scholars from across the empire and beyond its borders. The cities of *Eranshahr* were not merely administrative and commercial machines. They were places where ideas were tested, transmitted, and transformed.

Quick Summary

- Ctesiphon, founded during the Parthian era and expanded under the Sasanians, served as the empire's capital and one of the ancient world's largest cities until its fall to Arab Muslim forces in 637 CE.

- Ardashir I's foundation of Gōr exemplified Sasanian urban planning: circular in design, ideologically charged, and combining aesthetic ambition with military practicality.

- Sasanian cities functioned as administrative hubs, housing the officials, courts, and record-keepers through which the empire governed its vast territories.

- The empire's position between Rome and China made its cities critical nodes in the Silk Road trade network, generating wealth that drove urban growth and population expansion.

- Urban populations were ethnically and religiously diverse, including Zoroastrians, Jews, and Christians living within the same city walls.

- Sasanian architectural innovation - particularly in vaulted construction - left a legacy that passed directly into Islamic architecture and beyond.

- Cities like Gundeshapur were centers of intellectual life, hosting scholars in medicine, astronomy, and philosophy, making Sasanian urbanism a cultural as well as a political achievement.

The cities of the Sasanian Empire were, in the end, the empire's most durable argument for its own greatness. Armies could be defeated and dynasties could fall, but the urban forms, the architectural techniques, and the administrative traditions that *Eranshahr* developed did not disappear when Arab armies rode into Ctesiphon in 637 CE. They were absorbed, adapted, and carried forward - into the Abbasid caliphate, into Islamic civilization, and ultimately into the broader inheritance of the medieval world. The Sasanians built in order to last. In ways they could not have anticipated, they succeeded.

Chapter 16:
Art of Empire

Somewhere in the rocky hillsides of southwestern Iran, a king reaches down from horseback to receive a crown from a god. The stone has weathered nearly two thousand years of sun and wind, but the message remains unmistakable: this ruler does not merely govern by human consent. He governs by divine right, and the universe itself bears witness.

That image - Ardashir I accepting investiture from the great Zoroastrian divinity Ohrmazd - was not simply decoration. It was a declaration. When the Sasanians rose to power in 224 CE, displacing the Parthians and reclaiming the Persian heartland, they understood something that every ambitious empire eventually learns: conquest alone does not hold a civilization together. You need a story. And the Sasanians told theirs in stone, silver, and stucco, across palace walls and mountain faces, in hunting scenes and mythological tableaux that announced, again and again, who they were and why they deserved to rule.

Sasanian art is among the most politically sophisticated visual programs the ancient world produced. Spanning more than four centuries - from Ardashir I's founding of the empire in 224 CE to its collapse under the Arab conquests in 651 CE - it evolved from blunt assertions of royal power into a rich symbolic language that wove together religion, mythology, and statecraft. That language would outlast the empire itself, shaping the visual cultures of Byzantium, the Islamic world, and medieval Europe in ways that artists and patrons often never consciously traced back to their Persian source.

To understand the Sasanians, you have to look at what they made - and why they made it the way they did.

Rock Reliefs and Royal Imagery

Few artistic traditions announce themselves as boldly as the Sasanian rock relief. Carved directly into living cliff faces at sites across present-day Iran, these monumental images were not meant to hang in a gallery or sit in a treasury. They were meant to be seen by travelers, soldiers, pilgrims, and subjects - permanent, immovable proof that the king's authority was as solid as the earth itself.

Ardashir I, the empire's founder, established the template almost immediately. At Naqsh-e Rostam, near the ancient Achaemenid royal necropolis in Fars province, he commissioned a relief showing himself on horseback, receiving the ring of kingship from Ohrmazd, the supreme deity of Zoroastrian faith. Beneath the hooves of both figures lie defeated enemies - one of them widely identified as the last Parthian king, Artabanus IV. The composition is deliberate and layered: divine sanction above, military victory below, and the king at the center of both.

This was not a new idea in Persian art. The Achaemenids had used monumental relief carving at Persepolis and Bishapur to project royal power centuries earlier. But the Sasanians were not simply imitating their predecessors. They were consciously invoking them, claiming a cultural and dynastic continuity that legitimized their rule. By placing their own images near Achaemenid tombs and monuments, they inserted themselves into a longer story of Persian greatness.

Subsequent kings elaborated on the formula. Hunting scenes became a recurring motif, depicting rulers in pursuit of lions, stags, and wild boar - not merely as leisure activity, but as a demonstration of the king's strength, courage, and fitness to rule. Yazdgard I appears in artistic depictions slaying a stag, an image that carries both literal and symbolic weight: the king as master of nature, as protector of order against chaos. Bahram Gur, one of the most celebrated figures in Sasanian cultural memory, became so associated with the royal hunt that his name and image appear repeatedly in later Persian literature and art, long after the empire that produced him had vanished.

What makes these reliefs remarkable is not just their scale but their compositional confidence. Figures are rendered in profile or three-quarter view, with careful attention to the hierarchy of size - the king is always the largest figure, always the most central. Horses are shown in a flying gallop, a convention borrowed from earlier Near Eastern art but executed here with a dynamism that feels almost cinematic. Enemies, when they appear, are shown prostrate or trampled, their defeat rendered permanent in stone.

These were images designed to be read, not just admired.

Palaces and Architecture

If the rock reliefs were the empire's public face, its palaces were its interior life - spaces where the ideology of kingship was enacted in three dimensions, through ceremony, audience, and display.

Sasanian palace architecture is defined above all by the iwan: a massive vaulted hall, open on one end, that served as the monumental threshold between the outside world and the royal presence. At Ctesiphon, the Sasanian capital located on the Tigris River in present-day Iraq, the palace known as Taq Kasra preserves what remains of one of the largest brick-vaulted arches ever constructed in the ancient world. Its span reaches approximately 37 meters in height - an engineering achievement that would have been staggering to anyone approaching the court for the first time. That was, of course, entirely the point.

The iwan format solved a practical problem - how to create a large, column-free interior space in a region without abundant timber - while simultaneously creating a theatrical one. A visitor entering through the great arch would move from the heat and noise of the outside world into a cool, shadowed space of extraordinary height, then emerge into the royal audience hall beyond. Every step of that journey was calibrated to produce awe.

Interior surfaces amplified the effect. Sasanian palaces were decorated with carved stucco panels, painted frescoes, and mosaic floors, all featuring the same vocabulary of royal imagery found in the rock reliefs: hunting scenes, royal banquets, musicians, and mythological figures. Stucco allowed for a level of decorative detail impossible in stone - intricate floral patterns, interlocking geometric forms, and portrait roundels that covered walls and ceilings in a continuous visual program.

At Bishapur, founded by the great king Shapur I in the third century CE, excavations have revealed mosaic floors depicting court entertainments - musicians, dancers, and attendants arranged in registers that recall Roman provincial mosaics while remaining distinctly Persian in their iconographic choices. The presence of Roman-style mosaics at a Sasanian royal site is itself historically significant: Shapur I had defeated and captured the Roman Emperor Valerian in 260 CE, and Roman craftsmen were among the prisoners brought back to work on Persian building projects. Even in its decorative arts, the Sasanian palace was a record of conquest.

Symbolism in Art

Sasanian art was never purely decorative. Every element - the choice of animal, the arrangement of figures, the specific attributes held by a royal portrait - carried meaning that a contemporary viewer would have recognized immediately.

The investiture scene, repeated across multiple reigns, is perhaps the most theologically loaded image in the entire Sasanian repertoire. When a king receives the ring of kingship from Ohrmazd, the image asserts that royal authority flows directly from the divine order - that the king is not simply a powerful man but a cosmic figure, the earthly representative of truth and light in the Zoroastrian struggle against chaos and darkness. This was not mere flattery. It was a statement of political theology, one that had real consequences for how subjects understood their obligations to the crown.

Animals carried their own symbolic freight. The lion, appearing frequently in royal hunting scenes and on silver vessels, represented both the king's personal courage and his role as defender of civilization. The boar, associated in Zoroastrian tradition with the yazata Verethraghna - a deity of victory - appeared on royal crowns and personal seals as a mark of divine favor. Even the specific posture of a horse in a relief could signal whether the scene depicted a military triumph, a royal hunt, or a divine investiture.

Sasanian silverwork brought this symbolic vocabulary into a more intimate register. Silver vessels - bowls, plates, and ewers - were produced in workshops across the empire and distributed as royal gifts, diplomatic presents, and luxury goods for the aristocracy. Many feature mercury gilding and niello inlays, techniques that allowed craftsmen to create images of extraordinary detail and tonal richness. A silver plate showing a king hunting lions is not simply a beautiful object: it is a portable version of the same royal ideology expressed in the cliff-face reliefs, small enough to sit on a dining table but carrying the same political message.

Coins offered yet another medium. Silver drachms bearing the likeness of Bahram IV, for instance, circulated across the empire and beyond its borders, carrying the king's image - and by extension, his authority - into every market and treasury that handled Sasanian currency. In an era before mass media, coins were among the most widely distributed images in the world.

Art as Propaganda

It would be a mistake to read Sasanian art purely as aesthetic achievement. It was also, deliberately and systematically, an instrument of power.

Every major relief, every palace program, every coin issue was a political act. The choice of where to carve a relief - near an Achaemenid royal tomb, at a mountain pass, beside a sacred spring - was never accidental. These locations were chosen because they were already meaningful, already charged with religious or historical significance. By placing their images there, Sasanian kings were not just adding to the landscape; they were claiming it, rewriting its meaning in their own favor.

The revival of Persian cultural identity following Parthian rule gave this project particular urgency. The Parthians, though they had ruled Iran for nearly five centuries, were of Central Asian origin and had never fully embraced the Achaemenid legacy. The Sasanians, by contrast, came from Fars - the ancient Persian heartland - and made their connection to that tradition central to their self-presentation. Their art was part of a broader cultural argument: that they were the true heirs of Persian greatness, restoring what had been lost or diluted under foreign rule.

This argument was made visually as well as politically. By echoing Achaemenid compositional conventions - the processional frieze, the royal audience scene, the divine investiture - Sasanian artists created a visual continuity that reinforced dynastic legitimacy. A subject who recognized the debt to earlier Persian art would understand the implication: this king stands in a line of greatness stretching back to Cyrus and Darius.

At the same time, Sasanian art was not merely imitative. It developed its own distinctive aesthetic - more dynamic, more richly patterned, more theatrically composed than its Achaemenid predecessors - that reflected the empire's own cultural confidence. The hunting scenes, in particular, have an energy and immediacy that feels genuinely new, a visual language evolved to serve a civilization at the height of its power.

Influence Beyond Persia

When the Arab armies swept through the Sasanian Empire in the 640s CE, they did not erase what the Persians had built. They absorbed it.

Early Islamic art drew heavily on Sasanian visual conventions. The arabesque patterns that would become one of Islamic architecture's defining features owe a clear debt to Sasanian stucco decoration. The royal hunting scene, a staple of Sasanian silverwork, reappeared on Umayyad and Abbasid luxury objects with only minor modifications. Persian craftsmen, now working under new patrons, carried their techniques and iconographic habits into the new order.

The influence traveled westward as well. Byzantine art, already in dialogue with Sasanian Persia through centuries of trade and conflict, absorbed elements of Sasanian textile design, metalwork, and architectural ornament. Silk textiles woven in Sasanian workshops - featuring the paired animal roundels that became one of the era's most recognizable motifs - were traded across Eurasia and copied by weavers from Constantinople to China. Some of these textiles ended up as reliquary wrappings in medieval European churches, their Persian origins long forgotten by the monks who treasured them.

That is perhaps the most striking measure of Sasanian artistic achievement: its ideas outlived the empire that produced them by centuries, embedded in the visual cultures of civilizations that had, in some cases, actively conquered Persia. The Sasanians carved their power into stone - and into the imagination of the world that came after them.

- The Sasanian Empire (224-651 CE) developed one of the ancient world's most politically sophisticated artistic programs, using visual culture to assert royal authority and divine legitimacy.

- Rock reliefs carved into cliff faces at sites like Naqsh-e Rostam depicted kings receiving divine investiture from Ohrmazd, establishing a visual theology of royal power.

- Hunting scenes featuring rulers like Yazdgard I and the legendary Bahram Gur served as demonstrations of royal strength and cosmic order, not merely leisure.

- Palace architecture, exemplified by the great vaulted iwan at Ctesiphon, was designed to produce awe and reinforce the theatrical distance between the king and his subjects.

- Sasanian silverwork - plates, bowls, and ewers decorated with mercury gilding and niello inlays - carried royal iconography into aristocratic households and across trade networks.

- Coins bearing royal portraits, such as those of Bahram IV, distributed the king's image across the empire and into foreign markets, functioning as portable propaganda.

- Sasanian art consciously invoked Achaemenid precedents to claim cultural continuity and dynastic legitimacy, while developing its own dynamic and distinctive aesthetic.

- The empire's visual legacy persisted long after its fall, shaping early Islamic art, Byzantine decorative traditions, and medieval European textile design.

What the Sasanians understood - and what their art demonstrates with remarkable consistency - is that power needs a face. Not just an army, not just a bureaucracy, but a visible, legible, emotionally compelling image of itself. They built that image across four centuries, in media ranging from mountain-scale stone to palm-sized silver, and they built it so well that it survived the empire's destruction almost intact.

The civilizations that followed looked at what the Sasanians had made and recognized something worth keeping. That recognition is its own kind of testament - to the skill of the craftsmen, to the intelligence of the patrons who directed them, and to the enduring human need to make meaning visible.

Chapter 17:
Luxury and Identity

A silver fork could get you killed.

Not literally - not usually - but in the courts and counting houses of early modern Europe, the objects you owned, displayed, and used at table announced your place in the world with a precision that words rarely matched. Luxury was never simply about comfort or pleasure. It was a language, and those who spoke it fluently held power. Those who did not were reminded of that fact every time they sat down to dine.

Between 1500 and 1800, Europe underwent a transformation so sweeping that it reshaped nearly every dimension of human life. Explorers charted new continents. Scientists dismantled old cosmologies. Religious reformers tore apart the unity of Christendom. Centralized states gathered power that had once been scattered among feudal lords. And through all of it - the upheaval, the discovery, the violence, and the wonder - people continued to eat from plates, wear cloth, press seals into wax, and perform the elaborate rituals of court life. The material world did not stand apart from history. It *was* history, recorded not in ink but in silver, silk, and stone.

Luxury objects functioned in early modern European society not as mere decoration but as instruments of identity, power, and cultural meaning. Scholars working in the tradition of historian Natalie Zemon Davis, whose career helped establish material culture as a serious field of historical inquiry, have shown that understanding what people owned and how they used it is essential to understanding who they believed themselves to be. From the silverware on aristocratic tables to the gemstone seals pressed into diplomatic correspondence, luxury in this era was always doing more than one thing at once.

Silverware and Elite Culture

Few objects in early modern Europe carried more social weight than silver.

To own silver plate - dishes, cups, candlesticks, serving vessels - was to make a visible, permanent claim about your standing in the world. Silver did not rust, did not rot, and did not wear away easily. It lasted. In a society where status could be precarious, where fortunes rose and fell with harvests, wars, and royal favor, the permanence of silver offered something deeply reassuring. It said: *we have been here, and we intend to remain.*

At aristocratic tables across France, England, the Italian states, and the Habsburg territories, the display of silver was as important as the food it held. Guests were meant to notice. The gleam of a well-polished sideboard loaded with plate communicated wealth, taste, and lineage in a single glance. Hosts who could not match their rivals' silver risked something more than embarrassment - they risked being perceived as less than they claimed to be.

This was not vanity in any simple sense. Early modern elites operated in a world where appearance and reality were deeply intertwined. A nobleman who dressed poorly, dined from pewter, and kept a sparse table was not merely unfashionable. He was signaling weakness. Weakness invited challenge - from rivals, from creditors, from the crown itself. The investment in silver was, in this light, a rational one.

Silverware also carried meaning beyond the individual household. Gifts of silver plate moved between courts, between patrons and clients, between rulers and their favorites. A gift of silver was a gesture of alliance, of recognition, of obligation created and acknowledged. When a king presented a silver basin to a visiting ambassador, both parties understood the exchange as something far more consequential than a transaction. It was a statement about the relationship between their two worlds.

Craftsmen who produced these objects occupied a curious social position. Goldsmiths and silversmiths - the distinction between the two trades was often blurred in practice - were artisans, technically below the nobility they served. Yet their skill commanded respect, and the finest workshops in cities like Augsburg, Paris, and London attracted commissions from the highest levels of society. The objects they produced were not anonymous commodities. They were known works, associated with specific makers, and their quality reflected on the patron who owned them as much as on the craftsman who made them.

Silver also served as a store of value in an era before modern banking was fully established. A household's plate could be melted down in an emergency and converted to coin. This dual function - as display object and as liquid asset - made silver uniquely powerful among luxury goods. It was simultaneously a statement of wealth and a hedge against its loss.

Textiles and Global Influence

If silver announced status at home, cloth announced it everywhere.

Fabric was the most visible luxury of the early modern world, worn on the body, hung in windows, draped over furniture, and carried in processions. The quality, color, and origin of a person's clothing communicated their rank, their wealth, their religious affiliation, and sometimes their political allegiances - all before they had spoken a single word.

European textile production was already sophisticated by 1500, with major centers in Florence, Bruges, and later Lyon producing silks, velvets, and fine woolens that commanded high prices across the continent. But the period between 1500 and 1800 brought a dramatic expansion in the range and variety of fabrics available to European consumers, driven by the same forces of exploration and trade that were reshaping the wider world.

Contact with Asia, the Americas, and Africa introduced new fibers, new dyes, and new weaving traditions into European markets. Indian cotton, Ottoman silks, Chinese brocades - these goods arrived in European ports and immediately disrupted existing hierarchies of taste. What had been exotic became fashionable. What had been fashionable risked becoming ordinary. Elites responded by constantly raising the stakes, seeking out ever more refined, ever more expensive, ever more distant goods to mark their distance from those below them.

Sumptuary laws - regulations that attempted to restrict the wearing of certain fabrics and colors to specific social ranks - tell us a great deal about how seriously Europeans took the language of cloth. These laws were enacted across the continent, repeatedly, which itself suggests how difficult they were to enforce. As merchants grew wealthier and the middle ranks of society expanded, the old visual codes of dress became harder to maintain. A prosperous merchant's wife might wear silk that had once been reserved for noblewomen. The laws tried to hold the line. They rarely succeeded for long.

Color carried its own hierarchy. Certain dyes - particularly the deep crimson produced from kermes insects or, later, from cochineal imported from the Americas - were extraordinarily expensive and therefore extraordinarily prestigious. Purple had long been associated with imperial power. Scarlet became the color of cardinals. Black, paradoxically, became fashionable among the very wealthy in the sixteenth century precisely because achieving a true, deep black required expensive dye processes that cheaper fabrics could not replicate.

Textiles also moved ideas. Patterns, motifs, and techniques traveled along the same trade routes as the goods themselves, creating a visual culture that was genuinely global even when the people wearing the cloth had never left their home cities. A Venetian merchant wearing a robe of Ottoman-influenced fabric, embroidered with motifs that had traveled from Persia to Istanbul to the workshops of the Rialto, was participating in a world far larger than the one visible from his window.

Seals, Gems, and Personal Identity

A seal was a signature, a legal instrument, and a self-portrait all at once.

In an era when most official communication traveled by letter, and when the authenticity of that communication could mean the difference between alliance and war, between a binding contract and a forgery, the seal was indispensable. Pressed into wax at the foot of a document, it announced the identity of the sender with an authority that a written signature alone could not provide. Because seals were engraved on gemstones - carnelian, amethyst, onyx, rock crystal - they were also objects of beauty, worn on the finger or carried on the person as constant companions.

The imagery carved into a seal was chosen with care. Heraldic devices, mythological figures, portraits, mottoes - each element was selected to communicate something specific about the owner's identity, lineage, and values. A nobleman might choose an image that referenced his family's coat of arms. A humanist scholar might select a classical figure associated with wisdom or eloquence. A merchant might use a device that combined personal symbolism with a practical mark of commercial identity.

Gem engraving - the art of intaglio, in which images are cut into the surface of a stone - was a craft with roots in antiquity, and early modern collectors were acutely aware of this lineage. Ancient carved gems were among the most prized objects in Renaissance collections, valued both for their intrinsic beauty and for their connection to the classical world that humanist culture so admired. Owning an ancient gem was owning a piece of Rome or Greece - a tangible link to the civilizations that educated Europeans regarded as the foundation of their own.

Contemporary engravers worked in conscious dialogue with this ancient tradition, producing new gems that imitated antique styles while also serving the specific needs of their patrons. The line between an ancient gem and a skilled modern imitation was sometimes deliberately blurred, raising questions about authenticity and value that collectors found both troubling and fascinating.

Jewelry more broadly served as a portable form of wealth and identity. Rings, pendants, and brooches could be given as gifts, used as pledges, pawned in emergencies, and bequeathed to heirs. A piece of jewelry might carry a portrait miniature of a loved one, a lock of hair, a religious relic, or an inscription. These were not merely decorative objects. They were repositories of relationship and memory, worn close to the body as constant reminders of connection and obligation.

Court Life and Ceremony

All of these objects - the silver, the silk, the gemstone seal - found their fullest expression in the context of the court.

Early modern European courts were elaborate theaters of power, and the performance staged within them was never accidental. The rituals of court life - the processions, the banquets, the audiences, the hunts, the masques - were carefully choreographed displays in which every detail of dress, precedence, and material display carried meaning. To attend court was to participate in a continuous argument about hierarchy, loyalty, and legitimacy.

The French court at Versailles, developed under Louis XIV in the latter half of the seventeenth century, became the most influential model of this kind of ceremonial culture in Europe. But the impulse it represented - the use of spectacle and luxury to project royal power

- was visible across the continent long before Versailles was built. Italian Renaissance princes had understood it. Habsburg emperors had practiced it. Tudor monarchs of England had deployed it with considerable skill.

At court, the luxury objects discussed here were not merely owned - they were *performed*. A king who dined in public, surrounded by silver plate and attended by nobles competing for the honor of handing him his napkin, was staging a demonstration of power that no proclamation could match. The ceremony of the royal lever - the ritualized rising of the French king in the morning, attended by courtiers who jostled for the privilege of handing him his shirt - transformed the most mundane acts of daily life into political theater.

For those who attended court, mastering the codes of luxury and ceremony was not optional. It was survival. Knowing which fabric was appropriate for which occasion, understanding the precedence of seating at a royal banquet, recognizing the significance of a gift of jewelry from the monarch - these were the skills that separated the successful courtier from the embarrassing provincial. The court demanded constant investment in luxury goods, and it rewarded that investment with access to power.

Cultural Legacy

What does it mean that so much of early modern European identity was expressed through objects?

Scholars working in the tradition that Natalie Zemon Davis helped to shape have argued that material culture is not a superficial layer of history - it is one of the primary ways that human beings construct and communicate who they are. The silverware, the textiles, the gemstone seals, and the ceremonies of early modern Europe were not decorations on the surface of more important political or religious events. They were the medium through which those events were experienced and understood by the people who lived through them.

This period laid foundations that remain visible today. The luxury industries that developed in early modern Europe - in silk, in silversmithing, in fine jewelry - became the ancestors of the luxury goods sectors that still carry enormous cultural and economic weight. The idea that certain objects carry prestige, that ownership of beautiful things communicates something meaningful about the person who owns them, is not a modern invention. It is a very old human impulse, refined and elaborated across the three centuries examined here.

More broadly, the early modern period demonstrated that identity is never simply given - it is made, negotiated, and performed. The objects people chose to own and display were arguments about who they were and where they belonged in the world. That argument continues.

Quick Summary

- Luxury objects in early modern Europe (1500-1800) functioned as instruments of power, identity, and social communication, not merely as signs of wealth.

- Silver plate served simultaneously as a display of status, a medium of diplomatic exchange, and a store of liquid value in aristocratic households.

- European textile culture was transformed by global trade, as fabrics from Asia, the Americas, and the Ottoman world entered European markets and disrupted existing hierarchies of dress.

- Sumptuary laws attempted to restrict luxury consumption by social rank but were repeatedly enacted and repeatedly evaded, reflecting the difficulty of maintaining visual social hierarchies as merchant wealth grew.

- Gemstone seals combined legal function with personal identity, while jewelry more broadly served as portable wealth, memorial object, and gift of alliance.

- Court life provided the fullest context for the performance of luxury, with ceremonies at courts across Europe transforming material display into political theater.

- Scholars in the tradition of Natalie Zemon Davis have established material culture as a serious historical field, arguing that objects are essential evidence for understanding how identity was formed and expressed.

- Early modern luxury industries and the cultural values they embodied laid groundwork for ideas about prestige and material identity that persist into the present.

What people owned in early modern Europe was never just property - it was argument, allegiance, and autobiography compressed into silver and silk. The courts that staged these performances of luxury eventually gave way to revolutions that challenged the hierarchies they expressed. But the impulse to use beautiful objects to say something about who we are proved far more durable than any particular dynasty. It survived the guillotine. It survives still.

Chapter 18:
Minds of the Empire - Science, Medicine, and Learning

While armies clashed on the frontiers of the known world, something quieter and more lasting was happening in the heart of Persia. In a city called Gondeshapur, physicians debated the causes of disease in three languages. Astronomers charted the heavens using methods borrowed from Greece, India, and Babylon. Mathematicians worked through problems that no single civilization had solved alone. The swords would eventually rust. The knowledge endured.

A World That Thought as Well as Fought

The Sassanian Empire is most often remembered for its wars - the grinding campaigns against Rome, the cavalry charges, the sieges, the treaties signed and broken. But the empire that Ardashir I founded in 224 CE and that lasted until the Arab conquests of the seventh century was also one of the ancient world's most ambitious intellectual projects. Its rulers did not merely conquer territory. They collected ideas.

This was an empire that sat at the crossroads of civilizations. To the west lay the Roman and later Byzantine world, heir to Greek philosophy and medicine. To the east stretched India, with its own rich traditions in mathematics, astronomy, and healing. To the north and south moved merchants, missionaries, and refugees, each carrying fragments of knowledge from places the Sassanians had never ruled. Persia absorbed all of it - sometimes through war, sometimes through diplomacy, sometimes simply by offering scholars a place to work and a king willing to pay for results.

What emerged from this convergence was not merely a collection of borrowed ideas. It was something genuinely new: a tradition of synthesis, of taking the best thinking from multiple civilizations and forging it into something more powerful than any single source. That tradition would outlive the Sassanian Empire itself, flowing directly into the Islamic Golden Age that followed. To understand how the medieval Islamic world became the scientific center of the planet, you have to begin here, in a Persian city that most people have never heard of.

The Academy of Gondeshapur

Few institutions in the ancient world matched Gondeshapur for sheer intellectual ambition. Located in the southwestern province of Khuzestan - a fertile region that had long been a crossroads of trade and culture - the city was rebuilt and developed by Shapur I in the mid-third century CE, around 256 to 260 CE, following his campaigns against Rome. What Shapur brought back from those wars was not only plunder and prisoners. He brought people: engineers, craftsmen, physicians, and scholars captured or displaced from Roman-controlled territories.

Shapur I did not simply enslave his captives and put them to work on construction sites. He recognized that some of them carried knowledge worth more than gold, and he directed them toward pursuits that served the empire's intellectual ambitions. Gondeshapur grew around this influx of talent, becoming a city where Greek-speaking physicians worked alongside Persian scholars and Syrian translators.

Under Shapur II, who ruled from 309 to 379 CE, the city expanded further. Gondeshapur housed one of the ancient world's most sophisticated hospitals - a functioning medical institution where theory met practice in ways that were genuinely unusual for the era. Patients were treated, cases were observed, and the results fed back into the teaching. This was medicine as a discipline, not merely as a craft passed from father to son.

But it was under Khosrow I, who reigned from 531 to 579 CE, that Gondeshapur reached its peak. Khosrow was one of those rare rulers who combined military effectiveness with genuine intellectual curiosity. He did not simply fund scholars as a matter of prestige - he engaged with their work, debated philosophy at court, and made Gondeshapur the centerpiece of a deliberate policy of knowledge acquisition. By the sixth century, the academy had become the leading scientific institution in the known world, drawing talent from across the empire and beyond.

What made Gondeshapur extraordinary was not the size of its library or the number of its scholars, though both were considerable. It was the way it operated as a genuinely multicultural institution. Greek, Syriac, Persian, and Indian scholars worked in proximity, translating texts, comparing methods, and arguing over competing theories. A physician trained at Gondeshapur might know Hippocratic medicine, Ayurvedic practice, and Persian herbal tradition simultaneously. That breadth was not accidental. It was the point.

Medicine, Astronomy, and Mathematics

Medicine was the discipline in which Gondeshapur's synthesis proved most visible and most consequential. The academy's hospital - one of the earliest teaching hospitals in recorded history - operated on the principle that observation and experience should inform theory. Physicians were expected not only to read the classical texts but to test their conclusions against actual patients.

Greek medicine, particularly the Hippocratic and Galenic traditions, formed one pillar of Gondeshapur's medical knowledge. But Persian physicians did not simply copy what the Greeks had written. They compared it with Indian medical texts, incorporated local knowledge of plants and remedies, and produced something more comprehensive than any single tradition had achieved alone. The result was a medical culture that was, by the standards of the ancient world, remarkably empirical.

Astronomy followed a similar pattern, though the motives were partly practical. The Zoroastrian religious calendar depended on precise astronomical observation, and the movement of celestial bodies was tied to royal legitimacy in ways that made accuracy a political as well as a scientific matter. Persian astronomers drew on Greek astronomical models, particularly those derived from Ptolemy, but they also engaged seriously with Indian astronomical traditions, which had developed sophisticated mathematical tools for tracking planetary motion. Where these two traditions met at Gondeshapur, advances emerged that neither could have achieved independently.

Mathematics, too, benefited from this convergence. Indian numerical systems - including the place-value notation that would eventually become the Arabic numerals used across the world today - entered the Persian intellectual tradition through the channels that Gondeshapur helped to create. The implications were enormous, though they would take generations to fully unfold.

The Translation Movement: Greek and Indian Knowledge in Persia

Behind every act of intellectual synthesis at Gondeshapur stood an army of translators. These were not minor figures. They were among the most important scholars of their age, and the work they did - rendering Greek philosophical and scientific texts into Syriac and Persian, and Indian texts into Persian - was the essential precondition for everything else.

The translation movement in Persia predated Gondeshapur's peak, but it accelerated dramatically under Khosrow I. When the Byzantine Emperor Justinian closed the Platonic Academy in Athens in 529 CE, a number of its scholars - Neoplatonist philosophers who had nowhere else to go - made their way to the Sassanian court. Khosrow welcomed them. He was, by multiple accounts, genuinely interested in Greek philosophy, and the arrival of scholars who could teach it firsthand was an opportunity he seized.

These Greek scholars brought texts with them, and their presence at the Sassanian court created demand for more. Translation became a systematic enterprise, not merely an occasional act of curiosity. Works of Aristotle, Plato, Hippocrates, and Galen were rendered into languages that Persian and Syrian scholars could read and build upon. The knowledge did not simply sit in libraries - it entered the curriculum of Gondeshapur and shaped the education of the physicians, astronomers, and mathematicians who trained there.

Indian knowledge arrived through a different route. Khosrow I sent his court physician, a man named Burzoe, on a remarkable mission to India - not to conquer or to trade, but specifically to acquire knowledge. Burzoe returned with Indian medical texts and, famously, with the collection of fables known as the Panchatantra, which he translated into Middle Persian under the title Kalila wa Dimna. The medical texts enriched Gondeshapur's practice. The fables, in time, would travel westward into Arabic, Persian, and eventually European literature - one of the most traveled stories in human history.

This willingness to send a scholar across the subcontinent in search of knowledge says something important about Sassanian intellectual culture. Learning was not merely tolerated. It was actively pursued, funded, and treated as a matter of imperial interest.

Royal Patronage of Learning

None of this happened by accident. Gondeshapur existed because Sassanian kings decided it should exist, funded it, protected it, and in some cases personally participated in its intellectual life. Royal patronage was the engine that made the academy possible.

Shapur I's decision to settle captured Roman scholars in Gondeshapur rather than simply exploit them as laborers reflects a strategic calculation about the value of knowledge. Shapur II's expansion of the city continued this logic. But it was Khosrow I who turned royal patronage into something approaching a philosophy of governance.

Khosrow's court was a place where intellectual debate was expected and rewarded. He engaged directly with visiting philosophers, reportedly holding formal discussions on questions of ethics, cosmology, and the nature of the soul. He funded translations, supported physicians, and treated the advancement of knowledge as a legitimate function of imperial power - not merely as an ornament to royal prestige, but as something genuinely useful to the empire's strength and stability.

This model of royal patronage had a long afterlife. When the Abbasid caliphs established Baghdad as the center of a new Islamic empire in the eighth century, they did not invent the idea of a state-sponsored intellectual institution. They inherited it, largely from the Sassanian example. The famous House of Wisdom in Baghdad - the institution most closely associated with the Islamic Golden Age - drew directly on the Gondeshapur model, and in its early decades employed actual Gondeshapur scholars, many of whom relocated to Baghdad as the new center of power and patronage.

The transition was gradual. Gondeshapur did not collapse overnight. As Baghdad grew in wealth and influence, the gravitational pull of its patronage drew talent away from the older institution. By the ninth and tenth centuries, Gondeshapur had faded from its former prominence, its role absorbed by the new intellectual centers of the Islamic world.

What Persia Passed On to the Islamic World

The debt that the Islamic Golden Age owed to Sassanian Persia is difficult to overstate, and it is also frequently underestimated. When

Arab scholars in Baghdad began their own great translation movement in the eighth and ninth centuries - rendering Greek, Persian, and Indian texts into Arabic - they were not starting from scratch. They were continuing a process that Gondeshapur had already begun.

Many of the scholars who staffed the early Islamic intellectual institutions were Persian, or came from traditions shaped by Persian learning. The medical knowledge that flowed through Gondeshapur became the foundation of Islamic medicine. The astronomical methods developed at the academy fed directly into the work of Islamic astronomers who would eventually correct and extend Ptolemy's models. The mathematical traditions that converged at Gondeshapur - Greek geometry meeting Indian arithmetic - helped create the conditions for the development of algebra and the broader mathematical revolution of the Islamic Golden Age.

Persia did not simply preserve ancient knowledge and pass it on unchanged. It transformed that knowledge, tested it, combined it with traditions from multiple civilizations, and handed the result to the world that came after. That is a different kind of legacy than conquest, and in many ways a more durable one.

Key Takeaways

- **Gondeshapur**, rebuilt by Shapur I around 256-260 CE and expanded by subsequent rulers, became the ancient world's leading center of scientific and medical learning by the sixth century.

- **Khosrow I** (531-579 CE) was the academy's greatest royal patron, actively engaging with scholars, funding translations, and welcoming Greek philosophers expelled from Byzantium.

- **The academy's hospital** functioned as one of history's earliest teaching hospitals, combining Greek, Persian, and Indian medical traditions into a genuinely empirical practice.

- **Burzoe**, Khosrow's court physician, traveled to India specifically to acquire medical and literary knowledge - a mission that brought Indian texts into the Persian intellectual tradition.

- **The translation movement** at Gondeshapur rendered Greek, Syriac, and Indian texts into Persian, creating the multilingual scholarly culture that made synthesis possible.

- **Royal patronage** was the structural foundation of Sassanian intellectual life - learning was treated as a matter of imperial interest, not merely personal curiosity.

- **Gondeshapur's decline** came not from destruction but from competition: as Baghdad rose under the Abbasid caliphs, its patronage drew scholars away, and the academy's role was absorbed by the new Islamic intellectual centers it had helped to inspire.

The armies of the Sassanian Empire are long gone, their battles reduced to footnotes in the history of Rome and Byzantium. But the knowledge that moved through Gondeshapur - Greek medicine, Indian mathematics, Persian astronomy, all of it tested and combined and passed forward - shaped the world in ways that no military campaign ever could. What the scholars of the empire built outlasted the empire itself, flowing into the Islamic Golden Age and from there into the intellectual foundations of the modern world. That is the quiet power of ideas: they travel farther, and last longer, than any sword.

Part 6
Crisis, Collapse, and Legacy

Chapter 19:
Cracks in the System

Empires rarely fall from a single blow. They fracture slowly, unevenly, from the inside out, long before any external enemy delivers the final strike. The greatest threats to the Roman Empire did not arrive on horseback from beyond the Rhine or the Euphrates. They were already inside the walls, written into the very structure of how power was held, contested, and lost.

When the Center Cannot Hold

Rome in the third century CE looked, from a distance, much as it always had. Its legions still marched. Its cities still hummed with commerce. Its emperors still issued coins stamped with their own faces. But look closer, and the cracks were everywhere - in the rapid churn of men claiming the purple, in the treasury's growing desperation, in the restless ambitions of provincial generals who had learned that an army's loyalty could be bought, and that an emperor's throne was only as secure as his last victory.

What historians call the Crisis of the Third Century - roughly 235 to 284 CE - was not a single catastrophe. It was a sustained unraveling, a period of political and social upheaval so severe that it nearly destroyed the empire altogether. In the space of fifty years, Rome cycled through dozens of emperors, many of whom ruled for only months before being killed by rivals, mutinous soldiers, or both. Fragmentation became the norm. Breakaway states emerged at the empire's edges. Whole provinces slipped from central control.

Understanding how this happened - and why - requires looking not at any single villain or catastrophe, but at the structural pressures that had been building for generations. Succession crises, aristocratic rivalry, fiscal exhaustion, and religious tension all played their part. None alone would have been fatal. Together, they were.

Succession Crises and Dynastic Instability

No problem plagued Rome more persistently than the question of who came next.

The Roman Empire had never developed a reliable, institutionalized mechanism for transferring power. Unlike a monarchy with clear hereditary rules, Rome operated on a blend of adoption, military acclaim, senatorial approval, and raw force - a combination that worked tolerably well when strong emperors managed the transition, and catastrophically when they didn't. Every emperor's death, natural or otherwise, became a potential crisis.

During the third century, this weakness became impossible to ignore. Emperors rose and fell with dizzying speed. Some were capable soldiers elevated by their legions, only to be cut down the moment a rival general offered his troops a larger donative. Others were political figures backed by the Senate, lacking the military credibility to hold their position against the armies on the frontier. A few managed brief periods of stability before the cycle resumed.

The problem was self-reinforcing. Because the throne was never truly secure, emperors had powerful incentives to eliminate potential rivals - including capable generals who might otherwise have served the empire well. This created a climate of suspicion and political violence that made competent governance harder, not easier. Men who might have devoted their energies to administration or defense instead spent them watching their backs.

Dynastic instability also undermined the empire's ability to project consistent policy. A reign of two or three years was rarely long enough to see major reforms through. Infrastructure projects stalled. Military campaigns were abandoned mid-course. Alliances made with frontier peoples by one emperor were repudiated by his successor. The cumulative effect was an empire that could no longer act with the coherent long-term purpose that had once made it formidable.

What made this particularly dangerous was that Rome's neighbors noticed. The Sassanid Persians to the east and the Germanic confederacies to the north were not passive observers of Roman dysfunction - they were active opportunists, probing for weakness and pressing their advantages whenever Roman attention was divided. Internal instability had direct and immediate external consequences.

Aristocratic Power Struggles

Behind every emperor stood a network of powerful men whose support was essential and whose ambitions were never fully contained.

Rome's senatorial aristocracy had always occupied an uneasy position within the imperial system. Formally, the Senate retained enormous prestige and considerable administrative authority. In practice, real power had long since migrated to the emperor and his court. This tension - between the Senate's sense of its own importance and the reality of its diminished role - generated a persistent undercurrent of resentment and rivalry that periodically erupted into open conflict.

By the third century, a new layer of complexity had been added. Military commanders, many of them from provincial backgrounds rather than the traditional Roman aristocracy, had become the true kingmakers of the empire. It was the legions, not the Senate, that elevated and destroyed emperors. This shift created a fundamental competition between two power bases - the old civilian elite centered in Rome and the new military elite dispersed across the frontiers - neither of which could fully dominate the other.

The consequences were corrosive. Provincial governors with large armies under their command had both the means and the motive to challenge central authority. When an emperor appeared weak, or when the succession was disputed, the temptation to make a bid for power was often irresistible. Usurpations became so common during the third century that they ceased to be exceptional events and became, instead, a recurring feature of political life.

This aristocratic and military rivalry also distorted the empire's resource allocation in damaging ways. Emperors seeking to secure loyalty showered their supporters with gifts, land grants, and appointments - expenditures that drained the treasury and created a culture of patronage that rewarded political reliability over competence. The men who rose through this system were often skilled at surviving its treacherous dynamics, but not necessarily at governing the vast, complex entity they nominally controlled.

There was also a geographic dimension to these struggles. As the empire's frontiers expanded and then strained, power increasingly concentrated in the hands of men far from Rome - men whose primary loyalty was to their troops, their region, and their own advancement. The idea of a unified Roman ruling class, sharing common values and common interests, became harder to sustain as the third century wore on.

Economic Pressure and Fiscal Strain

Wars cost money. So do emperors who need to buy loyalty.

Rome's fiscal system had always depended on a combination of tribute from conquered territories, agricultural taxation, and the proceeds of commerce flowing through its vast trade networks. For centuries, this system generated enough revenue to fund the legions, maintain the roads and aqueducts, and sustain the elaborate apparatus of imperial administration. But by the third century, the model was under severe stress.

Continuous warfare on multiple frontiers was enormously expensive. Paying, equipping, and supplying the legions consumed a growing share of imperial revenue, and the military's political power meant that emperors could not easily reduce those costs without risking their own overthrow. The donatives - cash payments to soldiers at an emperor's accession or to secure their loyalty during crises - added further strain. Each new emperor who needed to buy his throne made the next fiscal crisis more likely.

To cover the gap between revenue and expenditure, Roman authorities resorted to a measure with predictable consequences: debasing the currency. Silver coins were progressively diluted with cheaper metals, reducing their intrinsic value while nominally maintaining their face value. In the short term, this allowed the state to pay its bills. In the longer term, it triggered inflation, eroded confidence in the monetary system, and disrupted the commercial networks that had been one of the empire's great economic strengths.

Taxation grew heavier as the fiscal situation worsened, falling disproportionately on the agricultural population - the peasants and small landowners who formed the backbone of the rural economy. As tax burdens increased, some abandoned their land rather than face ruin, reducing agricultural output and further shrinking the tax base. It was a vicious cycle, and Rome's administrators, for all their considerable abilities, could not find a way out of it.

Trade suffered as well. Political instability during the third century disrupted the long-distance commerce that had enriched the empire's cities and filled its coffers. Merchants needed predictable conditions, secure roads, and stable currency - none of which the crisis years reliably provided. Urban economies contracted. The middle layers of Roman commercial society, never as robust as those of later eras, thinned and weakened.

Religious Tensions

Alongside the political and economic pressures, a different kind of strain was building - one that cut across social classes and geographic boundaries, and that the empire's rulers found peculiarly difficult to manage.

Rome had always been, in religious terms, a remarkably capacious civilization. Its traditional approach to conquered peoples was to absorb their gods rather than suppress them, weaving local deities into the broad fabric of Roman religious life. This pragmatic pluralism had served the empire well for centuries, providing a kind of spiritual glue that helped bind diverse populations together under Roman rule.

But the rise of Christianity posed a challenge that this traditional approach struggled to accommodate. Unlike the mystery cults and regional religions that Rome had absorbed without difficulty, Christianity made exclusive claims - its adherents could not, in good conscience, offer the ritual sacrifices to the emperor's divine status that Roman civic religion required. This refusal was not merely a theological inconvenience. In Roman eyes, it was a political act, a rejection of the shared religious obligations that underpinned imperial unity.

Persecution of Christians was neither constant nor uniform across the third century, but it was real, and it reflected a genuine anxiety among Roman authorities about a movement that seemed to operate outside the normal channels of civic loyalty. The portrayal of Jesus as the "Good Shepherd" - a figure of care, protection, and spiritual authority - offered his followers an alternative center of allegiance, one that did not depend on the emperor's favor or the empire's stability.

At the same time, the empire's religious scene was fracturing in other ways. New cults competed for adherents. Traditional Roman religion, increasingly detached from genuine belief among the educated classes, struggled to provide the spiritual coherence it once had. The result was a society in which the old religious consensus was dissolving without any clear replacement - a condition that added to the general atmosphere of uncertainty and instability.

Religious tension, in this sense, was both a symptom and a cause of the empire's difficulties. It reflected the breakdown of the shared civic culture that had once held Rome together, and it made the task of rebuilding that culture harder.

Structural Weaknesses Laid Bare

What the Crisis of the Third Century ultimately revealed was not a set of problems that had suddenly appeared, but a set of weaknesses that had always been present - and that prosperity and military success had long concealed.

Rome's political system had never solved the succession problem. Its fiscal model depended on continuous expansion that could not continue indefinitely. Its military, essential to everything, was also the greatest single threat to political stability. Its religious framework, flexible as it was, could not easily accommodate movements that rejected the basic terms of Roman civic life.

None of these weaknesses was, in isolation, necessarily fatal. Empires have survived fiscal strain, religious conflict, and political instability. What made Rome's situation so dangerous was the way these pressures compounded each other - a political crisis making fiscal reform impossible, fiscal strain feeding military discontent, military instability preventing the consistent governance that might have addressed religious tensions, and so on in an interlocking web of dysfunction.

By the late third century, the empire had survived - but it was not the same empire. The reforms of Diocletian and later Constantine would stabilize the situation, but at the cost of fundamental changes to how Rome was governed, how its economy functioned, and how its identity was understood. The cracks had been papered over, not repaired.

Quick Summary

- Rome's Crisis of the Third Century (roughly 235-284 CE) was a period of intense political, economic, and social upheaval that nearly destroyed the empire.

- The lack of a reliable succession mechanism meant that every emperor's death risked triggering a new round of civil conflict and usurpation.

- Aristocratic and military power struggles fragmented authority and diverted resources from governance to political survival.

- Currency debasement and heavy taxation created a fiscal spiral that damaged trade, agriculture, and urban economies.

- Religious tensions - particularly around Christianity's refusal to participate in imperial cult worship - challenged the civic consensus that Roman rule depended on.

- These weaknesses were not new; the crisis revealed structural vulnerabilities that prosperity had previously concealed.

- Stabilization under later emperors came at the cost of fundamental changes to the empire's political and cultural character.

The cracks in Rome's system did not appear overnight, and they did not close easily. What the third century made visible - the fragility of power without legitimate succession, the danger of armies that answer to generals rather than institutions, the corrosive effect of fiscal desperation - were lessons that later empires would learn, forget, and learn again. History rarely offers clean warnings. More often, it offers exactly this: a slow accumulation of pressures, each manageable alone, that become something else entirely when they arrive together.

Chapter 20:
Revolution and Reform - The Mazdakite Crisis

Sometime in the late fifth century, a Persian preacher stood before the Sasanian emperor and told him that God wanted the rich to share everything they owned - including their wives.

What happened next nearly tore an empire apart.

A World Ripe for Disruption

The Sasanian Empire of the fifth and early sixth centuries was, by almost any measure, a civilization at its peak. Its armies had fought Rome to a standstill. Its merchants controlled the arteries of Silk Road trade. Its kings styled themselves "King of Kings," rulers of a realm that stretched from Mesopotamia to the edges of Central Asia. From the outside, it looked like permanence made flesh.

But inside, the empire was fracturing along lines of wealth and birth that had hardened over generations. A small aristocratic class - the great noble families, the Zoroastrian priesthood, the military elite - controlled vast estates and commanded the labor of those beneath them. Peasants worked land they would never own. Common soldiers fought wars that enriched men who never drew a sword. The gap between those at the top of Sasanian society and those at the bottom was not merely economic; it was encoded into law, ritual, and religion.

Into this world stepped Mazdak - a man whose ideas were so threatening to the established order that the empire's ruling class eventually united to destroy him, and whose memory was so dangerous that later sources worked hard to discredit everything he stood for.

What follows traces who Mazdak was, what he actually taught, why those teachings found such a powerful audience, and what the violent backlash against his movement revealed about the deep tensions running through one of the ancient world's most powerful states.

Who Was Mazdak?

Pinning down the historical Mazdak is harder than it sounds. Most of what survives about him comes from sources written by his enemies - Zoroastrian priests, Sasanian court historians, and later Islamic-era writers who inherited a tradition of treating Mazdakism as heresy and chaos. Separating the man from the polemics requires care.

What seems clear is that Mazdak was a Persian religious teacher active during the reign of the Sasanian king Kavad I, who ruled from approximately 488 to 531 CE, with a significant interruption in between. Mazdak operated within the broad tradition of Iranian religious thought, drawing on Zoroastrian cosmology - the eternal struggle between light and darkness, good and evil - but pushing its social implications in directions that orthodox Zoroastrianism had never gone.

He was not, as some later accounts suggested, a simple agitator or opportunist. By all indications, Mazdak was a sophisticated thinker who constructed a coherent theological framework to support his social program. His starting point was the Zoroastrian premise that the world was created good, that light and order were meant to prevail over darkness and chaos. His radical move was to argue that the existing social order - with its extremes of wealth and poverty, its rigid hierarchies of birth and privilege - was itself a form of darkness. Inequality was not natural or divinely sanctioned. It was a corruption, something that had crept into the world and needed to be corrected.

This was not merely a spiritual observation. Mazdak drew from it a practical conclusion: if God intended the world to be ordered and just, then human beings had an obligation to make it so. The hoarding of resources by the powerful was a sin against the divine order. Sharing - of food, of land, of property - was not charity. It was righteousness.

How Mazdak came to the attention of King Kavad I is unclear, but the encounter changed the course of Sasanian history. Kavad, facing serious political pressures from the great noble families who had grown powerful enough to depose kings - and who had, in fact, briefly deposed Kavad himself - found in Mazdak's movement something useful: a popular force that could be turned against the aristocracy. Whether Kavad genuinely believed in Mazdak's teachings or simply saw a political opportunity is a question historians have debated without resolution. What is certain is that for a period, the king lent the movement his support, and that support transformed Mazdakism from a religious sect into something approaching a state-sponsored revolution.

Radical Ideas and Social Reform

At the heart of Mazdakite teaching was a proposition that struck the Sasanian elite as nothing short of monstrous: that the resources of the earth belonged to all people equally, and that no one had the right to accumulate wealth while others starved.

This was, in the context of the ancient world, a genuinely radical claim. Most religious and philosophical traditions of the era accepted hierarchy as natural, even divinely ordained. The Zoroastrian system that underpinned Sasanian society organized people into distinct classes - priests, warriors, farmers, artisans - each with fixed roles and fixed relationships to power. Mazdak challenged the legitimacy of that entire structure.

His program, as best as can be reconstructed from hostile sources, called for the redistribution of grain and food stores held by the wealthy. He advocated for the breaking up of concentrated landholdings. He argued against the rigid hereditary privileges that determined a person's place in society from birth. In a world where a peasant's son was a peasant and a noble's son was a noble, this was explosive.

The most controversial element of Mazdak's teaching - and the one his enemies seized on most eagerly - was his position on women. Later sources, almost uniformly hostile, claimed that Mazdak advocated the communal sharing of women, treating them as property to be redistributed like grain or cattle. Modern historians treat these accounts with considerable skepticism. The claim served obvious polemical purposes: it painted Mazdakism as not merely socially disruptive but morally depraved, a movement that threatened the family itself. What Mazdak may actually have taught was something closer to a challenge to the institution of elite polygamy, in which powerful men accumulated large harems while ordinary men could not afford to marry at all. Whether this was a call for genuine equality in marriage or something more radical is impossible to determine with confidence from the surviving evidence.

What is not in doubt is the movement's popular appeal. Mazdak's followers - the Mazdakites - drew heavily from the lower strata of Sasanian society: peasants, urban poor, soldiers without prospects, people for whom the existing order offered nothing but continued subordination. When Kavad's royal backing gave the movement political cover, Mazdakites moved from preaching to action. Grain stores were opened. Noble estates were challenged. For a brief, extraordinary period, the social hierarchy that had structured Persian life for generations appeared genuinely unstable.

This was not a slow reform movement working through established channels. It was, by the standards of its time, a revolution - incomplete, contested, and ultimately short-lived, but a revolution nonetheless.

Elite Backlash and Royal Ambivalence

The Sasanian aristocracy watched the Mazdakite movement with a mixture of horror and fury. These were families who had held their positions for generations, who measured their worth in land and lineage, who understood the social order as the natural expression of divine will. A preacher telling their tenants that God wanted the grain redistributed was not a theological curiosity. He was an existential threat.

Their response was swift and coordinated. The great noble families, the Zoroastrian high priests, and the military commanders who had everything to lose from Mazdakite redistribution formed a unified opposition. They pressured Kavad. They worked to isolate the movement from royal protection. And when the opportunity came, they moved against it with lethal force.

Kavad's own position was deeply ambiguous throughout this period. He had used Mazdak and his followers as a counterweight against the nobles who had once deposed him, and the strategy had worked - for a time. But Kavad was also a king who needed his aristocracy to function. He needed their armies, their administrative networks, their cooperation in running an empire that stretched across thousands of miles. A permanent alliance with a movement that threatened to dissolve the social foundations of that aristocracy was not a sustainable political position.

There is also the question of his son. Khosrow, who would eventually succeed Kavad as Khosrow I - one of the most celebrated kings in Sasanian history - was a fierce opponent of Mazdakism. Whether Khosrow's hostility influenced his father's eventual turn against the movement, or whether Kavad had always intended to use Mazdak only as long as he was useful, is another question the sources leave unresolved.

What the period of royal ambivalence reveals is something important about how power actually worked in the Sasanian Empire. The king was not an absolute ruler in the modern sense. He operated within a web of obligations to the great families, the priesthood, and the military elite. A king who moved too far against those interests risked exactly what had happened to Kavad once before: deposition. Mazdak had given Kavad leverage. But leverage has limits.

Suppression and Its Consequences

The end of the Mazdakite movement came with brutal finality. Sometime in the early sixth century - the precise date is uncertain - Khosrow, acting either with his father's blessing or on his own authority, orchestrated a mass suppression of the Mazdakites. The sources describe executions on a large scale. Mazdak himself was killed, though accounts of the manner of his death vary and none can be fully trusted.

With the movement's leadership destroyed and royal protection withdrawn, Mazdakism collapsed as a political force. Its followers were persecuted. Its teachings were condemned by the Zoroastrian establishment. The redistribution of wealth that had briefly occurred was reversed wherever possible. The great families reclaimed their estates. The social order reasserted itself.

Yet the movement did not vanish entirely. Mazdakite communities survived in scattered form for centuries, persisting into the Islamic period as a minority religious tradition. The ideas Mazdak had articulated - about equality, about the injustice of concentrated wealth, about the obligation to share - proved harder to kill than the man himself. They surfaced periodically in later Iranian religious and political thought, echoing through movements that would come long after the Sasanian Empire had ceased to exist.

The immediate consequences of the suppression were significant. Khosrow I, who formally took the throne in 531 CE, launched a series of genuine administrative and fiscal reforms - reforms that addressed some of the underlying inequalities that had made Mazdakism so appealing in the first place. Tax systems were rationalized. Land surveys were conducted. The relationship between the crown and the peasantry was restructured in ways that gave ordinary farmers somewhat more stability. Historians have long debated whether these reforms were a response to the Mazdakite crisis - an attempt to drain the reservoir of popular grievance that had fed the movement - or simply part of Khosrow's broader program of imperial consolidation. The answer is probably both.

What the Crisis Revealed About the Empire

Strip away the theological controversy and the polemical distortions, and the Mazdakite crisis reads as a diagnostic moment - a point at which the underlying stresses of Sasanian society became impossible to ignore.

The movement's rapid spread told a clear story: enough people at the bottom of Sasanian society felt sufficiently aggrieved that a preacher promising divine sanction for redistribution could mobilize them into a force capable of threatening the established order. That kind of mass appeal does not emerge from nowhere. It requires genuine, widespread suffering - the kind that comes from watching grain stores fill while children go hungry, from watching noble families accumulate land that farmers work but will never own.

The elite's panicked response told an equally clear story. The speed and unity with which the aristocracy, the priesthood, and the military commanders moved against Mazdakism - despite their many other disagreements - revealed just how much the existing order depended on keeping the lower classes in their place. Mazdak had not merely threatened their wealth. He had threatened the entire conceptual framework through which they understood themselves and their right to rule.

And Kavad's ambivalence - his willingness to use the movement and then abandon it - revealed something about the structural constraints on royal power in the Sasanian system. Even a king could not simply choose the side of the poor against the rich. The machinery of empire required the cooperation of those who had the most to lose from equality.

Quick Summary

- Mazdak was a Persian religious teacher active in the late fifth and early sixth centuries CE, during the reign of Sasanian king Kavad I.

- His teachings drew on Zoroastrian cosmology to argue that social inequality was a corruption of the divine order, and that redistribution of resources was a religious obligation.

- Mazdakism gained extraordinary popular support among peasants, urban poor, and others excluded from Sasanian privilege.

- King Kavad I initially supported the movement as a political tool against the powerful noble families who had once deposed him.

- The Sasanian aristocracy, Zoroastrian priesthood, and military elite united in opposition, eventually securing the movement's violent suppression.

- Mazdak was killed, probably in the early sixth century, and the movement was crushed - though Mazdakite communities survived in scattered form for centuries.

- Khosrow I, who succeeded Kavad in 531 CE, implemented administrative and fiscal reforms that addressed some of the inequalities the crisis had exposed.

- The episode revealed deep structural tensions within the Sasanian Empire: between crown and aristocracy, between elite and commoner, between the ideology of divine order and the reality of concentrated power.

The Mazdakite crisis did not end inequality in the Sasanian Empire. It never came close. But it demonstrated something that every subsequent power in the region would eventually confront: that systems built on extreme concentration of wealth and rigid hereditary hierarchy carry within them the seeds of their own disruption.

Khosrow I's reforms bought the Sasanian state another century of relative stability. Whether they addressed the root of the problem, or merely postponed it, is a question the empire's eventual collapse would answer in its own time.

Chapter 21:
The Final Collapse

An empire that had endured for centuries - one that had absorbed barbarian invasions, survived civil wars, and outlasted plagues - did not die slowly. It collapsed in a matter of decades, and when the end came, it arrived with almost no resistance at all.

That fact alone should give us pause. Historians have spent generations debating the fall of great empires, searching for the single fatal wound. But the story of how the Sasanian Persian Empire came undone in the seventh century is not a story of one catastrophic blow. It is a story of accumulation - of wars that drained the treasury, plagues that emptied the cities, rulers who could not hold power long enough to matter, and then, at the worst possible moment, an enemy unlike anything the empire had faced before.

By the time the Arab armies arrived, the Sasanian Empire was already a hollow structure. The walls still stood. The titles still existed. But the will, the wealth, and the administrative coherence that had made the empire formidable for four centuries had quietly bled away. What followed was less a conquest than a collapse that had been building for decades.

This chapter traces that collapse from its origins in the final, ruinous war with Byzantium, through the internal chaos that followed, to the Arab conquests that finished what exhaustion had started - and asks the question that still haunts historians: why did one of the ancient world's great powers fall so completely, and so fast?

The Last War with Byzantium

For most of their shared history, the Sasanian Empire and the Byzantine Empire had fought each other to a standstill. Their wars were costly, bloody, and ultimately inconclusive - a rhythm of advance and retreat that neither side could decisively break. But the war that began in the early seventh century was different in kind. It was not a border dispute or a contest over a single city. It was an existential struggle, and it left both empires shattered.

The conflict escalated into one of the most destructive wars the ancient Near East had ever seen. Sasanian forces pushed deep into Byzantine territory, capturing Jerusalem in 614 and seizing the True Cross - a symbolic blow of enormous psychological weight in the Christian world. Egypt fell. Anatolia was overrun. For a moment, it appeared that the Sasanian Empire might finally achieve what it had long sought: the permanent destruction of its western rival.

It did not last. The Byzantine Emperor Heraclius launched a stunning counteroffensive that reversed nearly every Sasanian gain. By 628, the war had turned completely. The Sasanians were driven back, their armies exhausted and their treasury emptied. The True Cross was returned. The territories were lost. And the Sasanian king, Khosrow II - the monarch who had overseen the empire's greatest expansion - was overthrown and killed by his own son.

That moment of internal rupture was decisive. The war had not merely drained resources; it had destroyed the political legitimacy of the ruling dynasty. Khosrow's death triggered a succession crisis of extraordinary violence. In the decade that followed, the Sasanian throne changed hands more than a dozen times. Generals fought generals. Nobles conspired against kings. Children were crowned and then murdered. The administrative machinery that had held the empire together - the tax collectors, the provincial governors, the military commanders - lost its coherence almost entirely.

Byzantium had won the war. But the victory was pyrrhic. Both empires had spent themselves into ruin fighting each other, and neither had the strength left to face what was coming next.

Exhaustion, Plague, and Instability

War was not the only force tearing the empire apart. Beneath the political chaos ran deeper currents of exhaustion - demographic, economic, and environmental - that had been building for generations.

Plague had visited the ancient world repeatedly, and its effects were rarely short-lived. The Antonine Plague, identified by historians as likely smallpox, had devastated the Roman world between 165 and 180 A.D., killing millions and disrupting the agricultural and economic systems that sustained urban civilization. The Sasanian world was not immune to such epidemics, and repeated outbreaks across the late antique period thinned populations, reduced agricultural output, and strained the tax base that funded armies and administration alike.

Climate played a role as well. The Roman Climate Optimum - a period of relatively warm, stable weather that had supported agricultural productivity across much of the ancient world from roughly 550 B.C. to A.D. 150 - had long since ended. The centuries that followed brought greater instability: cooler temperatures, irregular harvests, and the cascading social pressures that follow when food becomes uncertain. These were not dramatic, visible catastrophes. They were slow, grinding pressures that weakened the foundations without announcing themselves.

Economic mismanagement compounded the damage. The Sasanian state, like many ancient empires, depended on a steady flow of revenue from territorial expansion and trade. When conquests slowed and trade routes became disrupted, the financial pressure fell on existing populations - heavier taxation, debasement of currency, neglect of infrastructure. Resources that might have maintained roads, irrigation systems, and frontier defenses were diverted elsewhere or simply lost to corruption.

Provincial governors enriched themselves at the expense of the populations they administered. The military, underpaid and undersupplied, became unreliable. At the center of it all, a succession of short-lived rulers - many of them installed by powerful noble factions and removed just as quickly - could not provide the sustained direction that a crisis of this magnitude demanded.

By the 630s, the Sasanian Empire was not merely weakened. It was ungoverned. The throne was occupied, but it commanded little loyalty and less obedience. The army existed on paper more than in practice. And the population, ground down by decades of war, taxation, and uncertainty, had largely lost the will to defend a state that had ceased to protect them.

The Arab Conquests

Into this vacuum came the armies of Islam.

The speed of the Arab conquests remains one of the most remarkable military phenomena in recorded history. Within a generation of the Prophet Muhammad's death in 632, Arab forces had swept across the Arabian Peninsula, conquered the Levant, taken Egypt, and shattered the Sasanian Empire entirely. What had taken Rome centuries to build, the Arab armies dismantled in years.

The conquests were not simply a matter of religious fervor, though faith was undeniably a powerful motivating force for the early Muslim armies. Arab forces were disciplined, mobile, and tactically sophisticated. They moved quickly across terrain that heavier armies struggled to cross. They exploited local grievances, offering terms of surrender that were often more attractive than continued resistance under a failing imperial government.

The Sasanian Empire, for its part, could barely mount a coherent defense. The Battle of al-Qadisiyyah, fought around 636, was the decisive engagement. Sasanian forces, though numerically significant, were poorly coordinated and led by commanders who owed their positions to political survival rather than military competence. The Arab victory was total. The Sasanian capital of Ctesiphon fell shortly afterward - a city that had stood as one of the great urban centers of the ancient world, home to magnificent palaces and the accumulated wealth of centuries.

The last Sasanian king, Yazdegerd III, fled eastward, seeking refuge and support that never materialized. He spent years as a fugitive in his own empire, appealing to provincial governors who either could not or would not help him. He was killed in 651, reportedly by a local miller - an ignominious end for the heir of a dynasty that had once challenged Rome as an equal.

What made the Arab conquests so complete was not simply military superiority. It was the absence of any meaningful resistance infrastructure. The Sasanian administrative system had collapsed. The army had fragmented. The nobility was divided and demoralized. Local populations, many of them exhausted by decades of misrule and heavy taxation, did not rise en masse to defend a government they no longer trusted. Some communities actively cooperated with the new rulers, calculating that Arab governance could hardly be worse than what they had endured.

The conquests also benefited from the simultaneous weakness of Byzantium. The two great powers that might have checked each other - and that had, for centuries, kept the Arab world contained - were both spent. There was no counterweight left.

Why the Empire Fell So Quickly

Speed is the thing that demands explanation. Empires do not usually vanish in a decade. What made the Sasanian collapse so total, so fast?

Part of the answer lies in the nature of ancient imperial administration. Sasanian power depended on a relatively small number of key institutions - the monarchy, the Zoroastrian priesthood, the military aristocracy, and the provincial governorship system. When the monarchy destabilized after the death of Khosrow II, it pulled the other institutions down with it. There was no redundancy, no alternative power structure that could absorb the shock and maintain order.

Part of the answer also lies in the loss of what might be called institutional will. Research on Rome's decline offers a useful parallel: when territorial conquests slowed and economic inflows decreased, the empire's capacity to maintain itself deteriorated. The same dynamic applied to the Sasanians. Decades of inconclusive war, financial mismanagement, and administrative corruption had eroded the confidence - among both rulers and ruled - that the empire was worth defending.

Frustration and disillusionment are harder to measure than armies or tax revenues, but they matter enormously. When a population stops believing that its government can protect and provide for it, the social contract that sustains political authority quietly dissolves. By the 630s, that dissolution was well advanced across the Sasanian world.

Climatic stress and plague had weakened the demographic and agricultural foundations. Internal power struggles had destroyed political coherence. The last war with Byzantium had consumed whatever military and financial reserves remained. The Arab conquests did not cause the collapse - they revealed it.

End of the Dynasty

The Sasanian dynasty had ruled Persia since 224 A.D., when Ardashir I defeated the last Parthian king and established a new Persian empire that would endure for more than four centuries. At its height, it had been a civilization of genuine brilliance - a patron of art, architecture, and learning, a rival to Rome and Byzantium, a crossroads of trade between East and West.

Its end was neither glorious nor gradual. Yazdegerd III, the last king, never commanded the loyalty of his empire in any meaningful sense. He was a young man thrust onto a collapsing throne, moving from province to province in search of support that never came. His death in 651 - alone, far from his capital, killed not in battle but in obscurity - marked the formal end of the dynasty.

No successor state emerged. No Sasanian rump kingdom survived in the mountains or the eastern provinces. The dynasty simply ceased to exist, absorbed into the new Islamic order that was remaking the political map of the ancient world.

What remained was memory: the Persian language, Persian administrative traditions, Persian art and literature - all of which would profoundly shape the Islamic civilization that replaced the Sasanian state. The conquerors, in many ways, became the conquered, absorbing Persian culture even as they dismantled Persian political power. That cultural persistence is perhaps the most remarkable legacy of a dynasty that, in political terms, vanished almost without trace.

Quick Summary

- The final war between the Sasanian Empire and Byzantium (early seventh century) left both powers militarily and financially exhausted, with neither capable of defending against new threats.

- Khosrow II's death triggered a catastrophic succession crisis; the Sasanian throne changed hands more than a dozen times in a single decade.

- Decades of plague, climatic instability, economic mismanagement, and administrative corruption had hollowed out the empire's capacity to govern and defend itself.

- Arab armies that arrived in the 630s were disciplined, mobile, and tactically effective - but they exploited a collapse already well underway.

- The Battle of al-Qadisiyyah (c. 636) broke Sasanian military resistance; the fall of Ctesiphon followed shortly after.

- Yazdegerd III, the last Sasanian king, died as a fugitive in 651, ending a dynasty that had ruled Persia for more than four centuries.

- The speed of the collapse reflected not just military defeat but the disintegration of political legitimacy, institutional coherence, and popular will to resist.

- Persian culture - language, administration, art - survived the political collapse and deeply shaped the Islamic civilization that followed.

Four centuries of Persian imperial power did not end because the Arabs were invincible. They ended because the Sasanian Empire had, piece by piece, dismantled the conditions of its own survival. What the Arab conquests delivered was a final verdict on a process that war, plague, misrule, and exhaustion had already set in motion.

The world that emerged from the ruins was not simply a Persian world under new management. It was something genuinely new - an Islamic civilization that stretched from the Arabian Peninsula to the edges of Central Asia, carrying within it the deep imprint of the Persian world it had absorbed. Empires end. What they leave behind rarely does.

Chapter 22:
The Empire That Never Truly Died

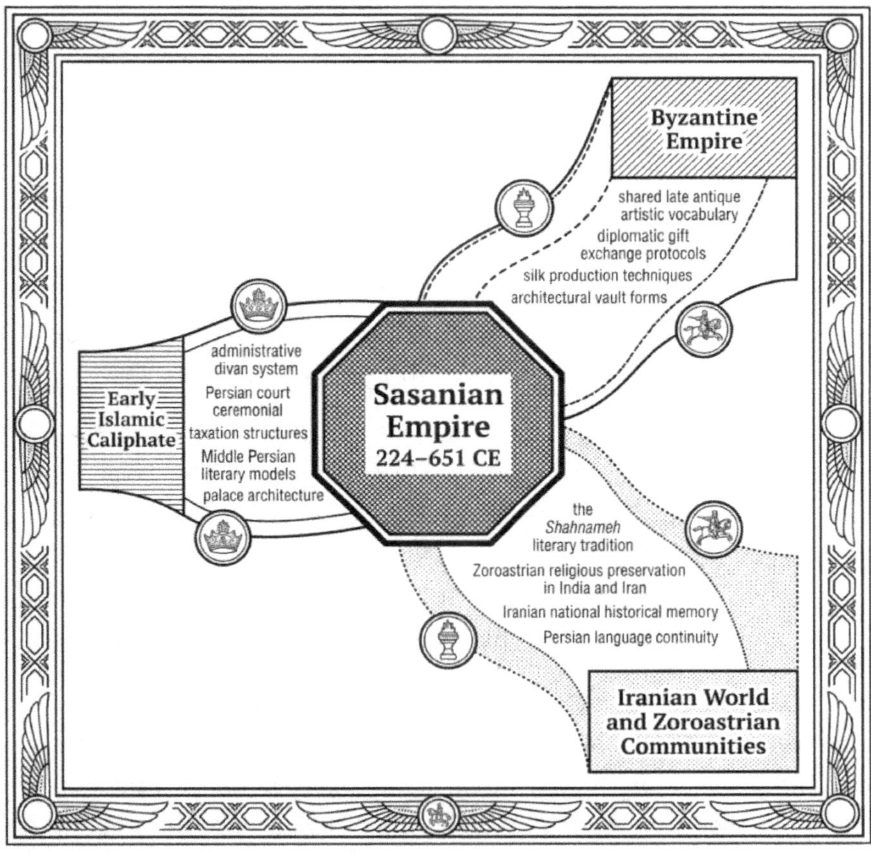

What the Sasanians Left Behind: Their Legacy Across Three Civilizations

When the last Sasanian emperor, Yazdgerd III, was murdered by a miller near the city of Merv in 651 CE, it seemed like a definitive ending. A dynasty that had ruled Persia for over four centuries - that had built cities, codified laws, patronized artists, and held the Roman

Empire at bay - was gone. The throne was empty. The fire temples were threatened. The old order had collapsed.

Except it hadn't. Not really.

A Disappearance That Wasn't

Empires rarely vanish cleanly. They collapse at the top - a dynasty ends, a capital falls, a last emperor flees - but the structures beneath them, the habits of governance, the patterns of culture, the assumptions about how power should look and feel, those things are far more durable than any throne. The Sasanian Empire, which stretched from its founding under Ardashir I in 224 CE to its final unraveling under the Arab Conquest in the seventh century, is one of history's most striking examples of this phenomenon.

On paper, the Sasanians were finished. Yazdgerd III spent his final years as a fugitive, moving from province to province as Arab armies consolidated their hold over Persian territory. He died not in battle, not in a palace, but in obscurity - killed by a local man in a provincial backwater. There was no dramatic last stand, no final proclamation. Just an ending that felt more like a fading.

But what followed was not erasure. It was absorption. The Arab conquerors who dismantled the Sasanian state found themselves inheriting something they hadn't entirely planned for: a sophisticated, deeply embedded civilization that had been governing complex territory for centuries. Administrators, scribes, tax collectors, artists, and priests - the human machinery of the Sasanian world - did not simply disappear because the dynasty had. They adapted. And in adapting, they transformed the world that replaced them.

This is the story of how an empire that officially ended in 651 CE continued to shape the world for centuries afterward - through its bureaucratic DNA, its artistic vocabulary, its religious memory, and its enduring hold on Persian identity.

Survival of Administrative Systems

Conquering a territory is one thing. Governing it is another entirely.

When Arab armies swept through the Sasanian heartland in the 630s and 640s CE, they were extraordinarily effective as a military force. As administrators of a vast, agriculturally complex, multilingual empire, they were starting almost from scratch. The Sasanians, by contrast, had spent four centuries building one of the ancient world's most sophisticated bureaucratic systems - a layered apparatus of provincial governors, tax assessors, scribes, and record-keepers that kept grain moving, revenues flowing, and irrigation networks functioning across enormous territory.

The practical solution was obvious, even if it carried a certain irony: keep the system running, and keep the people who knew how to run it.

Sasanian administrative practices were integrated into early Islamic governance with remarkable speed. Coinage provides one of the clearest examples. In the years immediately following the conquest, Arab rulers continued to mint coins that were visually and structurally derived from Sasanian models. The forms were familiar, the weights were familiar, and the populations using them barely noticed the transition at the mint. Currency, after all, only works if people trust it - and trust, in the ancient world, was built through familiarity.

The Zoroastrian-derived social hierarchy that had organized Sasanian society also persisted longer than might be expected. Sasanian social structure divided the population into distinct classes - priests, warriors, scribes, and commoners - a hierarchy rooted in Zoroastrian doctrine and centuries of institutional practice. This framework did not evaporate overnight. In the early Islamic period, these social categories continued to shape how communities organized themselves, how status was understood, and how local administration functioned, even as the theological justification for the system officially changed.

Perhaps most consequentially, Sasanian expertise in agricultural administration - particularly the management of the elaborate irrigation systems that made Mesopotamian agriculture possible - was simply too valuable to discard. Fortified Sasanian administrative sites were eventually abandoned as the conquest reshaped settlement patterns, but the knowledge embedded in those systems, the understanding of water rights, land tenure, and seasonal management, survived in the people who had always maintained them.

What the Arab conquerors built was not a replacement for the Sasanian administrative world. It was, in large part, a continuation of it, wearing new religious and political clothing.

Influence on Early Islamic Rule

The Sasanian legacy did not merely survive the conquest. It actively shaped what came after.

As the early Islamic caliphates expanded and consolidated power, they faced the perennial challenge of imperial governance: how do you project authority across vast distances, collect taxes efficiently, maintain armies, and administer justice in territories with radically different languages, customs, and traditions? The Sasanians had grappled with exactly these questions for four hundred years, and their answers - encoded in administrative practice, court ceremony, and bureaucratic culture - were available to anyone willing to learn from them.

The surviving Sasanian nobility played a crucial role in this transmission. Rather than being systematically eliminated or marginalized, many members of the Persian aristocracy found ways to integrate themselves into the new order. They brought with them not just administrative competence but a whole set of assumptions about how a great empire should look and feel - the ceremonies of court, the protocols of audience, the architecture of power. In the ancient and medieval world, the theater of rulership was inseparable from rulership itself. Appearance was substance.

This influence reached its peak with the Abbasid Caliphate, which came to power in 750 CE and shifted the center of Islamic power eastward, toward the old Sasanian heartland. The Abbasids drew heavily on Persian administrative models, employing Persian-speaking bureaucrats and viziers who carried Sasanian traditions of governance into the new imperial framework. The figure of the powerful vizier - the chief minister who managed the day-to-day machinery of empire while the caliph held symbolic and religious authority - owed much to Sasanian precedent.

Later, the Samanid dynasty, which emerged in the ninth and tenth centuries CE, made the connection explicit. The Samanids consciously positioned themselves as heirs to the Sasanian tradition, working to revive Persian language, culture, and administrative practice as markers of legitimate authority. They were not trying to restore the Sasanian Empire - that was gone. They were doing something subtler and more lasting: using Sasanian memory as a foundation for a new Persian cultural identity within the Islamic world.

The conquest had changed the religion of Persia. It had not erased its institutional memory.

Cultural and Artistic Legacy

Beyond governance, the Sasanians left behind a visual and artistic vocabulary that proved remarkably persistent.

Sasanian art - characterized by elaborate metalwork, intricate textile patterns, royal hunting scenes, and monumental rock reliefs - did not simply stop being produced when the dynasty fell. Its motifs and techniques migrated into Islamic art, carried by the same craftsmen and workshops that had always produced them. The hunting imagery that had adorned Sasanian silver plates, depicting kings on horseback pursuing lions and stags, reappeared in early Islamic decorative arts, stripped of its explicitly royal Zoroastrian symbolism but retaining its visual power and prestige.

Textile production offers another vivid example. Sasanian weavers had developed sophisticated techniques for producing richly patterned silks, and these textiles were luxury goods traded across the ancient world. The workshops that produced them continued operating after the conquest, and Sasanian textile patterns - roundels containing paired animals, stylized trees, and royal figures - spread westward into Byzantine art and eastward into Tang dynasty China, carried along the Silk Road long after the empire that originated them had ceased to exist.

Architectural influence was equally durable. The Sasanian iwan - a large vaulted hall open on one side - became a fundamental element of Islamic architecture, appearing in mosques, palaces, and caravanserais across the Islamic world. Visitors to great medieval Islamic buildings were, in a real sense, standing inside a space whose basic form had been developed by Sasanian architects centuries earlier.

These were not accidental survivals. They reflected the depth and sophistication of Sasanian material culture - a civilization that had developed distinctive and highly refined answers to questions of beauty, prestige, and representation. When the Islamic world needed its own artistic vocabulary, it drew extensively on what was already there.

Memory, Myth, and Iranian Identity

Perhaps the most enduring legacy of the Sasanian Empire is the most intangible: the role it came to play in Persian memory and self-understanding.

Ardashir I, who overthrew the Parthians and founded the dynasty in 224 CE, had positioned the Sasanians as restorers of ancient Persian glory - heirs to the Achaemenids, defenders of Zoroastrian tradition, rightful rulers of Iran. This was a powerful founding myth, and it did not lose its potency when the dynasty fell. If anything, the Arab Conquest intensified it. Persia had been conquered before and had absorbed its conquerors. The memory of Sasanian greatness became a resource for those who wanted to assert that Persian civilization was not finished - that it had a past worth honoring and a future worth building.

This memory was cultivated deliberately. Persian-speaking poets, scholars, and rulers in the post-conquest centuries returned repeatedly to Sasanian themes, figures, and imagery. The great Persian epic tradition drew on Sasanian-era stories and legends, weaving them into a narrative of Iranian identity that transcended any particular dynasty or religion. The kings of the Sasanian period became legendary figures - idealized, mythologized, and made to carry the weight of a civilization's self-image.

Yazdgerd III, the last emperor, is a particularly poignant case. His flight and death were, in historical terms, a story of defeat and collapse. But in Persian memory, he became something more complex - a symbol of loss, certainly, but also of the endurance of what he represented. The Sasanian world he embodied did not simply accept its own disappearance.

The Samanids understood this dynamic and exploited it skillfully. By championing the Persian language and Sasanian cultural memory, they helped ensure that Persian identity survived - and eventually flourished - within the Islamic world. The result was not a restoration of the Sasanian Empire but something arguably more resilient: a cultural tradition that could persist without a state to protect it.

Why the Sasanians Still Matter

Four centuries of rule leave marks that outlast the rulers. The Sasanian Empire shaped the administrative foundations of the early Islamic caliphates, provided the artistic vocabulary for a new civilization, and gave the Persian-speaking world a reservoir of memory and identity that proved extraordinarily durable.

Their story challenges a common assumption about conquest - that the winners write the future as well as the history. In the case of the Sasanians, the conquered shaped the conquerors as profoundly as they were shaped by them. Arab armies that swept through Persia in the seventh century won the military contest decisively. But the civilization they encountered did not simply yield. It adapted, persisted, and ultimately left its fingerprints on everything that came after.

Quick Summary

- The Sasanian Empire lasted from 224 to 651 CE, ending with the Arab Conquest and the death of Yazdgerd III.

- Sasanian administrative systems - including coinage, tax structures, and agricultural management - were absorbed into early Islamic governance rather than replaced.

- Surviving Sasanian nobility helped transmit Persian administrative and court culture into the Abbasid Caliphate and subsequent Islamic dynasties.

- The Samanid dynasty consciously revived Sasanian cultural traditions as a foundation for Persian identity within the Islamic world.

- Sasanian artistic motifs - hunting imagery, textile patterns, and architectural forms like the iwan - persisted and spread widely through Islamic and broader Eurasian art.

- Persian cultural memory transformed Sasanian kings into legendary figures, anchoring a durable sense of Iranian identity that survived the loss of the empire itself.

- The Sasanian legacy demonstrates that civilizations can outlast the states that created them, shaping the world through culture, memory, and institutional inheritance long after their political structures have collapsed.

Empires end. Civilizations are harder to kill. The Sasanians built something that proved far more durable than any dynasty - a way of governing, a way of making beauty, and a way of understanding what it meant to be Persian. Those things passed through the rupture of conquest and came out the other side, changed but intact. What followed the Sasanians was not simply an Islamic world built on the ruins of a Persian one. It was, in many ways, both at once - and that complexity is still visible today in the art, the institutions, and the identity of the region.

Conclusion:
Legacy of a Forgotten Superpower

Some empires are remembered for how they fell. Others for what they became. The Sasanian Empire, which ruled for more than four centuries across one of the most strategically vital regions on earth, managed both - collapsing dramatically under the weight of Arab conquest, yet surviving in a quieter, more durable form through the art, science, governance, and cultural memory it left behind. To understand the Sasanians only through their fall is to miss the point entirely. Their real story is what they built, and how much of it endured.

The Sasanian World in Retrospect

When Ardashir I overthrew the Parthian king Artabanus IV around 224–225 C.E. and declared himself ruler of a new Persian empire, he was doing something more than seizing power. He was making a claim about identity - that Iran had a continuous civilization worth reviving, worth defending, and worth projecting outward into the world.

That claim turned out to be one of the most consequential in the ancient world.

For over four centuries, the empire Ardashir founded stood as a superpower in every meaningful sense. It matched Rome and then Byzantium in military reach. It developed sophisticated administrative systems capable of governing vast, ethnically diverse populations. It produced art of extraordinary refinement - metalwork, textiles, and monumental rock reliefs that announced Persian greatness to anyone who passed through its territories. And it cultivated a religious and intellectual culture, rooted in Zoroastrianism, that shaped how millions of people understood the cosmos, morality, and the proper relationship between rulers and the divine.

What makes the Sasanian achievement remarkable is not just its scale but its self-consciousness. This was an empire that knew it was an empire. Sasanian rulers styled themselves as heirs to the ancient Achaemenids - the dynasty of Cyrus and Darius - and invested heavily in the idea that Persian civilization had a destiny. That sense of historical purpose animated everything from royal architecture to court poetry to the careful preservation of older Iranian traditions.

Yet for all its grandeur, the Sasanian Empire remains curiously underappreciated in the popular imagination of the West. Ask most educated readers to name the great powers of late antiquity, and they will reach for Rome, Byzantium, perhaps the Gupta Empire of India. The Sasanians - who fought Rome to a standstill, captured a Roman emperor, and built cities that rivaled Constantinople in size and sophistication - rarely make the list.

Part of this neglect is a matter of geography. Sasanian Persia sits at the edge of the mental map most Western readers carry. Part of it is a matter of sources: much of what we know about the Sasanians comes filtered through the accounts of their enemies or through later Islamic scholarship, which had its own reasons for framing the pre-Islamic Persian past in particular ways. And part of it is simply the accident of historical memory - which civilizations get written about, taught in schools, and turned into popular narratives, and which ones quietly recede.

The Sasanians receded. But they did not disappear.

Lessons from a Forgotten Superpower

Every great civilization teaches something to those willing to look closely. What the Sasanians teach may be more relevant now than at any point in the past several centuries.

The first lesson is about resilience. Sasanian Persia was not a static entity. Over four centuries it absorbed shocks - military defeats, internal rebellions, dynastic crises, and the constant pressure of powerful neighbors - and adapted. Its administrative structures proved flexible enough to govern enormous distances without the kind of rigid centralization that makes empires brittle. When one approach failed, another was tried. The empire that existed in the seventh century C.E. looked quite different from the one Ardashir had founded, and that capacity for evolution was a feature, not a flaw.

The second lesson concerns the relationship between culture and power. Sasanian rulers understood, with unusual clarity, that military dominance alone does not sustain an empire. Culture does. They invested in art, in religious institutions, in the patronage of learning, and in the physical infrastructure of cities and roads. They created a Persian identity robust enough to survive even the empire's political collapse - which is precisely what happened. When the Arab armies swept through in the seventh century, they destroyed the Sasanian state. They could not destroy the Persian cultural inheritance.

That inheritance proved extraordinarily durable. Persian language, literature, artistic conventions, and administrative practices did not vanish with the empire. They were absorbed, adapted, and carried forward - first by the early Islamic caliphates, which relied heavily on Persian bureaucratic expertise to govern their own vast territories, and later by dynasties across Central Asia, South Asia, and the broader Islamic world. The Sasanian legacy became, in a very real sense, the skeleton beneath the body of medieval Islamic civilization.

The third lesson is about the cost of exhaustion. By the early seventh century, the Sasanian Empire had fought itself nearly to death. Decades of brutal warfare with Byzantium had drained its treasury, depopulated its frontier regions, and destabilized its political center. A rapid succession of rulers - some reigning for only months - left the imperial administration in chaos. When the Arab armies arrived, they did not face the Sasanian Empire at its height. They faced an empire already staggering.

This is a pattern that recurs across history with uncomfortable regularity. Great powers rarely fall to external enemies alone. They fall when internal exhaustion meets external pressure at precisely the wrong moment. The Sasanians are a case study in how even the most sophisticated and durable civilizations can become vulnerable when they lose the capacity to renew themselves.

Bridge Between Ancient and Medieval Worlds

One of the most important - and least appreciated - roles the Sasanian Empire played was that of a bridge.

Bridges are easy to overlook. We notice the shores on either side; we cross the span without thinking much about what holds us up. Remove the bridge, and the crossing becomes impossible.

Sasanian Persia connected the ancient world to the medieval one in ways that shaped the trajectory of human civilization. The intellectual traditions of Greece, translated and preserved in Sasanian academies like the famous school at Gundeshapur, passed through Persian hands before reaching the scholars of the early Islamic world who would transmit them to medieval Europe. Mathematics, astronomy, medicine, philosophy - the great inheritance of ancient learning did not travel in a straight line from Athens to Baghdad. It passed through Persia.

Gundeshapur deserves particular attention. Under Sasanian patronage, this city in southwestern Iran became one of the most important centers of learning in the late ancient world. Scholars from across the empire - and from beyond it, including Greek-speaking refugees fleeing Byzantine religious persecution - gathered there to study and translate texts. The hospital and medical academy at Gundeshapur ranked among the most sophisticated institutions of their kind anywhere. When the early Abbasid caliphs sought to build their own intellectual culture, they drew directly on the Gundeshapur tradition.

This transmission was not passive. Persian scholars did not simply copy and pass along what they received. They synthesized, critiqued, and expanded it. The Sasanian intellectual tradition was an active participant in the development of human knowledge, not merely a relay station between earlier and later civilizations.

Sasanian artistic conventions tell a similar story. The visual language developed under Sasanian patronage - the treatment of royal figures, the use of hunting scenes as symbols of royal power, the intricate geometric and floral patterns of Persian decorative art - flowed directly into early Islamic art and architecture. Scholars can trace specific motifs from Sasanian metalwork and textiles into the decorative programs of the great early mosques and palaces of the Islamic world. The aesthetic vocabulary of medieval Islamic civilization was, in significant part, a Sasanian vocabulary.

In governance, too, the Sasanian model proved influential. Persian administrative practices - the use of trained bureaucrats, sophisticated tax systems, and formal court protocols - were adopted and adapted by the early caliphates. The Persian concept of the just ruler, a king who governs in accordance with divine order, protects his subjects, and maintains the cosmic balance, became deeply embedded in Islamic political thought, where it shaped ideas about legitimate authority for centuries.

The Sasanians in the Iranian Story: A Series Perspective

For Iranians, the Sasanian Empire occupies a particular place in the national imagination - one that is both celebrated and complicated.

Ardashir I's founding of the empire in 225 C.E. is remembered as a moment of restoration: the revival of Iranian greatness after centuries of Parthian rule, which many later Iranian historians characterized as a period of fragmentation and cultural stagnation. Whether or not that characterization is entirely fair to the Parthians, the Sasanian period came to be seen as a golden age - a time when Iranian civilization reached a kind of apex before the disruption of the Arab conquest.

That conquest, which unfolded across the middle decades of the seventh century, brought Islam to Iran and ended the Zoroastrian state. For later generations of Iranians, this transition carried enormous emotional and cultural weight. The pre-Islamic past became, in certain traditions, a source of pride and longing - a civilization of great sophistication that had been interrupted, though not erased.

This tension between pre-Islamic and Islamic identity has run through Iranian culture for more than a millennium. It surfaces in literature, in art, in political discourse, and in the way Iranians have periodically returned to the Sasanian period as a touchstone for questions about who they are and where they came from. The great Persian epic the *Shahnameh*, composed by the poet Ferdowsi around the turn of the first millennium C.E., drew heavily on Sasanian-era traditions and legends to construct a vision of Iranian identity that explicitly bridged the pre-Islamic and Islamic worlds.

Within the arc of this series, the Sasanian Empire represents a culmination and a turning point simultaneously. It is the moment when the long story of ancient Iranian civilization - stretching back through the Achaemenids and beyond - reaches its final pre-Islamic expression. And it is the moment when that civilization, transformed but not destroyed, begins its long journey into a new world.

Understanding the Sasanians is not simply an exercise in recovering a forgotten chapter of ancient history. It is essential to understanding how Iran became what it is - how a civilization absorbed one of the most dramatic ruptures in its history and emerged, centuries later, with its cultural identity not only intact but enriched.

The Sasanian legacy is not a relic. It is a living inheritance.

What Comes Next

Every ending is also a beginning. The collapse of the Sasanian Empire in the seventh century did not close the Iranian story - it opened a new chapter, one defined by the encounter between Persian civilization and the rapidly expanding world of Islam.

That encounter was not simply a story of conquest and submission. It was a story of negotiation, synthesis, and transformation. Persian culture shaped early Islam as profoundly as Islam reshaped Persian culture. The result was something genuinely new: an Islamicate civilization in which Persian language, aesthetics, administrative practice, and intellectual tradition played a foundational role.

Cities that rose across the Iranian plateau in the early Islamic centuries were not simply Arab outposts planted in conquered territory. They were Persian cities, living within a new political and religious framework but drawing on deep wells of local tradition. The scholars, poets, and administrators who built early Islamic civilization were, in many cases, Iranians - men and women who carried the Sasanian inheritance forward into a new world.

What comes next, in the broadest sense, is the story of how that inheritance traveled. How Persian became the literary language of an empire stretching from Anatolia to India. How Sasanian artistic motifs appeared on the walls of mosques from Spain to Central Asia. How the administrative genius of Persian bureaucrats helped hold together caliphates that would otherwise have fragmented under their own weight.

The Sasanians did not survive as an empire. But the world they built - the ideas, the art, the institutions, the sense of identity - proved more durable than any army or any dynasty. That is the final, most important lesson of a civilization too long forgotten: that what endures is rarely what was meant to last, and that the most powerful legacies are often the ones no one planned.

Quick Summary

- Ardashir I founded the Sasanian Empire around 225 C.E., deliberately positioning it as a revival of ancient Iranian civilization and the heir to the Achaemenid tradition.

- For over four centuries, the Sasanians functioned as a genuine superpower, matching Rome and Byzantium militarily while developing sophisticated systems of governance, art, and religious culture.

- The empire's collapse in the seventh century resulted from a combination of prolonged warfare with Byzantium and the sudden pressure of Arab conquest - a pattern of external pressure meeting internal exhaustion.

- Despite political collapse, Sasanian cultural achievements proved extraordinarily durable, flowing directly into early Islamic civilization through art, administrative practice, intellectual tradition, and language.

- Institutions like the academy at Gundeshapur served as critical transmission points for ancient learning, helping preserve and develop Greek, Persian, and Indian intellectual traditions that would later shape medieval Islamic and European scholarship.

- The Sasanian period occupies a central place in Iranian cultural memory, representing both a golden age and a point of rupture - a tension that has animated Iranian identity for more than a thousand years.

- The true legacy of the Sasanian Empire is not found in its political history alone, but in the civilizational inheritance it passed forward: a Persian identity robust enough to survive conquest and continue shaping the world long after the empire itself was gone.

Some empires leave behind monuments. The Sasanians left behind something harder to see and far more difficult to destroy: a way of understanding the world, a set of aesthetic instincts, a tradition of governance and learning that proved capable of outlasting the political structures that had carried it. Their empire fell. Their civilization did not. In that distinction lies one of the most instructive stories the ancient world has to offer - one whose echoes have not yet finished sounding.

A Note on Sources

The Sasanian Empire lasted over four centuries and rivaled Rome at its height - yet it left behind almost no literature of its own. This section explains, in plain terms, how historians piece together one of antiquity's most powerful empires from sources that are fragmentary, hostile, or written centuries after the fact. It is not a bibliography. It is an honest account of how we know what we know - and where we are still guessing.

The Source Problem: Why So Little Survived

The Sasanians were prolific administrators and enthusiastic patrons of learning, but almost nothing they wrote in Middle Persian survives from the imperial period itself. The royal archives of Ctesiphon were lost after the Arab conquests. The great fire temples, which served as repositories of sacred and administrative texts, did not survive the transition to Islamic rule intact. What remains is a scattered residue: a handful of inscriptions, administrative seals, coins, rock reliefs, and religious texts preserved by the Zoroastrian community in later centuries - most of them copied and edited long after the empire fell.

This is a problem unique to the Sasanians among the great ancient empires. Rome left libraries. Egypt left papyri. Mesopotamia left clay tablets. Persia left stone. The rock reliefs at Naqsh-e Rostam and Taq-e Bostan are extraordinary documents of royal ideology - but they tell us what kings wanted posterity to see, not how the empire actually functioned. Reconstructing Sasanian history therefore requires working across multiple languages, traditions, and disciplines simultaneously, and accepting a higher-than-usual margin of uncertainty.

Byzantine and Roman Accounts: Useful but Hostile

The most detailed narrative accounts of Sasanian history come from the empire's greatest enemy. Byzantine historians - Procopius, Agathias, Theophylact Simocatta, Menander the Guardsman - wrote extensively about Persia, particularly during the wars of the sixth and seventh centuries. They are indispensable. They are also deeply unreliable on anything touching Persian internal affairs.

Byzantine writers observed Persia from the outside, through the lens of a civilization that regarded itself as the rightful heir of Rome and the Sasanians as its permanent adversary. They are sharper on military campaigns and diplomatic negotiations - subjects they witnessed or had access to firsthand accounts of - than on Persian religion, society, or administration, which they frequently misrepresent or caricature.

Procopius is a brilliant prose stylist and an acute observer of war; he is also a man who had strong political axes to grind and limited sympathy for Persian perspectives. Readers of this book should understand that when we describe Sasanian military strategy or frontier policy in the western chapters, we are often working primarily from sources written by the people the Sasanians were fighting.

Armenian chronicles - particularly the works of Elishe and Lazar P'arpec'i - offer a partial corrective. Armenia sat between the two empires and had intimate knowledge of both. Armenian writers are especially valuable on Sasanian religious policy and the experience of Christian communities within the empire.

Early Islamic Sources: Rich but Retrospective

The richest body of material on the Sasanian Empire was written in Arabic and Persian after the empire's fall - sometimes centuries after. The great historian al-Tabari, writing in the ninth and tenth centuries, devoted substantial sections of his universal history to the Sasanian kings, drawing on earlier Arabic compilations that themselves drew on Persian oral traditions and now-lost administrative records. The *Shahnameh* of Ferdowsi, composed around 1000 CE, preserves a vast legendary tradition about Sasanian kings - particularly Khosrow I and Khosrow II - that blends history, myth, and Iranian national memory in ways that are often impossible to disentangle.

These sources are extraordinarily valuable and must be used with care. They were written by scholars operating in an Islamic cultural framework, often with an interest in presenting the Sasanian period as a kind of pre-Islamic golden age that Islam then superseded or fulfilled. They also had access to Persian traditions and texts that no longer exist, which means they sometimes preserve genuine historical memory in forms we cannot verify. The rule of thumb used throughout this book: Islamic sources are most reliable on administrative structures, royal genealogies, and cultural life; least reliable on religious details and the internal politics of the pre-Islamic court.

Archaeology, Coins, and Material Culture

Where written sources fail, objects speak. Sasanian archaeology has advanced dramatically in the past half century, and it has repeatedly corrected or complicated what texts alone suggested. Excavations at Ctesiphon, Bishapur, Firuzabad, and numerous smaller sites have revealed the physical shape of Sasanian urban life - palace layouts, fire temple architecture, water management systems, market infrastructure. Surveys of the Diyala plain in Iraq have documented the extraordinary irrigation networks that made Mesopotamia one of the most productive agricultural regions in the ancient world.

Coins are among the most reliable documents the Sasanians left behind. Every king issued coins with his portrait and name, and the numismatic sequence is nearly complete. Coins tell us about royal titulature, the chronology of reigns, religious symbolism, and - when studied in bulk - patterns of economic activity and monetary policy.

They are particularly useful for the chaotic seventh century, when the literary record becomes confused and the coin evidence helps establish the sequence of rulers during the empire's final collapse.

Sasanian silver plate - the luxurious dishes and ewers that circulated as elite gifts and symbols of status - has been found from Britain to China, a material trace of the empire's global reach. Seals and sealings from administrative contexts, now distributed across museum collections worldwide, offer glimpses into bureaucratic practice that no text describes directly.

What We Can and Cannot Know

Readers should approach this book knowing that some of its confident-sounding assertions rest on thin foundations. We know a great deal about how Sasanian kings presented themselves - the rock reliefs are unambiguous on this. We know considerably less about how ordinary people experienced the empire, what women's lives looked like in practice, or how provincial administration actually functioned day to day. The closer we get to the center of power, the more evidence we have; the further we move toward the margins - rural communities, non-Zoroastrian minorities, the empire's eastern frontiers - the more we are extrapolating from limited data.

This is not a reason for despair. It is a reason for honesty. The Sasanian Empire is one of the most rewarding subjects in ancient and late antique history precisely because so much remains to be discovered. New inscriptions surface. Archaeological sites yield new data. Syriac Christian texts are still being edited and translated. The picture presented in this book is the best current account - not the final one.

Chronology

All dates CE unless otherwise noted.

Year	Ruler / Event	Significance
224	Ardashir I defeats Artabanus IV at the Battle of Hormozdgan	End of Parthian rule; founding of the Sasanian Empire
224–240	Reign of Ardashir I	Consolidation of empire; centralization of power; early promotion of Zoroastrianism
240–270	Reign of Shapur I	First great Sasanian king; defeats three Roman emperors including Valerian (260)
260	Capture of Emperor Valerian at the Battle of Edessa	Unprecedented humiliation of Rome; commemorated in rock reliefs at Naqsh-e Rostam
270–293	Reigns of Hormizd I, Bahram I, Bahram II, Bahram III, Narseh	Period of internal consolidation; execution of Mani (274–277)
293–302	Reign of Narseh	Defeated by Rome; Treaty of Nisibis (299) - major Sasanian territorial concession
309–379	Reign of Shapur II	Longest-reigning Sasanian king; recovery of lost territory; persecution of Christians; wars with Constantius II
363	Death of Emperor Julian during invasion of Persia; Treaty of 363	Rome cedes Nisibis and other territories; major Sasanian diplomatic victory
379–383	Reign of Ardashir II	
383–388	Reign of Shapur III	
388–399	Reign of Bahram IV	

399–420	Reign of Yazdegerd I	Relative toleration of Christians; engagement with Roman diplomacy
420–438	Reign of Bahram V (Bahram Gur)	Legendary king; wars with Huns; celebrated in later Persian literature
438–457	Reign of Yazdegerd II	Renewed persecution of Christians and Jews; wars with Eastern Rome
457–459	Reign of Hormizd III	
459–484	Reign of Peroz I	Catastrophic wars against the Hephthalite Huns; Peroz killed in battle (484)
484	Battle of Herat	Death of Peroz; Sasanian Empire pays tribute to Hephthalites for decades
484–488	Reign of Balash	
488–496	Reign of Kavad I (first reign)	Rise of Mazdak movement; Kavad deposed by nobility
496–498	Reign of Zamasp	Installed by nobles opposing Kavad and Mazdakism
498–531	Reign of Kavad I (second reign)	Suppression of Mazdakite movement; major administrative reforms; wars with Byzantium
c. 524–528	Suppression of the Mazdakite movement	Mass execution of Mazdakites under Khosrow; social order restored
527	Justinian becomes Byzantine Emperor	Beginning of era of intensified Roman-Persian conflict
531–579	Reign of Khosrow I (Anushirvan)	Greatest Sasanian ruler; sweeping reforms of taxation, military, and administration; patronage of learning; Gondeshapur flourishes
540	Khosrow I sacks Antioch	Major Persian victory; resettlement of Syrian population in Persia
562	Fifty Years' Peace with Byzantium	Temporary stabilization of the western frontier

572	Renewed war with Byzantium	
579–590	Reign of Hormizd IV	
590–628	Reign of Khosrow II (Parviz)	Initial glories followed by catastrophic overreach; conquest of Egypt, Syria, Palestine (611–619); ultimate defeat
614	Persian capture of Jerusalem; removal of the True Cross	High point of Sasanian expansion westward
619	Persian occupation of Egypt	Maximum territorial extent of the Sasanian Empire
622–628	Byzantine counteroffensive under Heraclius	Dramatic reversal; Persian armies defeated; Khosrow II assassinated (628)
628	Assassination of Khosrow II	Beginning of catastrophic succession crisis
628–632	Rapid succession of at least eight rulers	Empire in freefall; central authority collapses
632	Yazdegerd III becomes last Sasanian king	Last attempt to stabilize the empire
633–651	Arab Muslim conquests of Persia	Battle of al-Qadisiyyah (636); fall of Ctesiphon (637); Battle of Nahavand (642)
651	Death of Yazdegerd III	End of the Sasanian dynasty
Parallel world events		
313	Edict of Milan	Christianity legalized in Roman Empire
376–410	Gothic migrations and sack of Rome	Accelerating fragmentation of Western Roman Empire
476	Fall of Western Roman Empire	Byzantine Empire continues as Sasanian counterpart

527–565	Reign of Justinian I	Last great effort to reunite Roman Empire; major Byzantine-Persian wars
570	Birth of Muhammad	
618	Tang Dynasty founded in China	Height of Silk Road connectivity
622	The Hijra; beginning of Islamic calendar	
632	Death of Muhammad; beginning of the Rashidun Caliphate	Arab conquests begin

Bibliography and Further Reading

This bibliography is a guide for readers who want to go further, not an exhaustive academic apparatus. Entries are organized by part of the book, with a short note on what each work offers and who it is best suited for. Works marked with ★ are the most accessible starting points for non-specialist readers.

Primary Sources

These are the ancient and medieval texts on which our knowledge of the Sasanian Empire is primarily based. Most are available in English translation.

Procopius, *Wars* and *Secret History* - The Byzantine historian's accounts of the Persian wars of the sixth century are the fullest narrative source for that period. Sharp on military affairs, hostile on Persian character. The Loeb Classical Library editions are the standard scholarly text; the Penguin translation of the *Secret History* is accessible and entertaining.

al-Tabari, *The History of al-Tabari*, vols. 4–5 (SUNY Press translations) - The indispensable Islamic-era source on Sasanian kings, drawing on Persian oral tradition and lost administrative records. Invaluable and must be read critically. The SUNY series provides facing-page annotation.

Ferdowsi, *Shahnameh: The Persian Book of Kings* - The great Iranian national epic, composed c. 1000 CE, preserving legendary and semi-historical traditions about Sasanian kings. Dick Davis's translation (Penguin Classics) is outstanding. Not a historical source in the strict sense - essential reading nonetheless. ★

Elishe, *History of Vardan and the Armenian War* (Harvard University Press translation) - The most important Armenian source on Sasanian religious policy and the experience of Christian communities under Sasanian rule. Covers the fifth century in particular.

The *Denkard* - A vast ninth-century Zoroastrian compendium preserving much older religious and administrative material. No complete English translation exists; partial translations and summaries are available in the scholarly literature.

Ammianus Marcellinus, *Res Gestae* - The last great Latin historian covers Persian affairs in the fourth century, including the campaigns of Julian. The Loeb edition is standard; the Penguin translation is readable. ★

Further Reading by Part

Introduction and General Works

- Touraj Daryaee, *Sasanian Persia: The Rise and Fall of an Empire* (I.B. Tauris, 2009) - The best single-volume scholarly overview available in English. Concise, authoritative, and accessible to serious general readers. ★

- Zeev Rubin and Ursula Diehl (eds.), *The Cambridge Companion to the Age of Attila* - Useful for placing the Sasanians in their late antique context.

- Richard Frye, *The Heritage of Persia* (Weidenfeld & Nicolson, 1963) - An older but still valuable survey of Iranian civilization from the Achaemenids through the Islamic period, providing long-run context for the Sasanian chapters. ★

- Encyclopaedia Iranica (online at iranicaonline.org) - The essential reference work for all things Iranian. Free, peer-reviewed, and updated regularly. The single most useful resource for readers wanting to go deeper on any topic in this book. ★

Part 1 - Origins and Rise

- Vesta Sarkhosh Curtis and Sarah Stewart (eds.), *The Age of the Parthians* (I.B. Tauris, 2007) - Essential background on the Parthian system the Sasanians overthrew.

- Rahim Shayegan, *Arsacids and Sasanians: Political Ideology in Post-Hellenistic and Late Antique Persia* (Cambridge University Press, 2011) - Detailed scholarly analysis of how the Sasanians constructed their legitimacy against Parthian precedent.

- Touraj Daryaee, *Šahrestānīhā ī Ērānšahr: A Middle Persian Text on Late Antique Geography, Epic, and History* - Primary source in translation; useful for understanding how Sasanians conceived of their own territory.

Part 2 - Building the Imperial Machine

- Josef Wiesehöfer, *Ancient Persia from 550 BC to 650 AD* (I.B. Tauris, 2001) - Excellent on administrative and social structures across the Iranian imperial tradition. ★

- Maria Macuch, *Rechtskasuistik und Gerichtspraxis zu Beginn des siebenten Jahrhunderts in Iran* - The foundational work on Sasanian law; in German, but the essential reference for the legal chapter.

- Philippe Gignoux, *Catalogue des sceaux, camées et bulles sasanides* - The standard reference on administrative seals as evidence for bureaucratic structures.

Part 3 - Religion, Society, and Power

- Prods Oktor Skjærvø, *The Spirit of Zoroastrianism* (Yale University Press, 2011) - The best accessible introduction to Zoroastrian belief and practice. ★

- Shaul Shaked, *Dualism in Transformation: Varieties of Religion in Sasanian Iran* (School of Oriental and African Studies, 1994) - Essential on the diversity of religious life within the empire.

- Jacob Neusner, *A History of the Jews in Babylonia*, 5 vols. - The authoritative study of the Jewish community under Sasanian rule; detailed and indispensable for Chapter 8.

- Iain Gardner and Samuel Lieu (eds.), *Manichaean Texts from the Roman Empire* (Cambridge University Press, 2004) - Useful primary sources for understanding Manichaeism and its persecution.

- Maria Macuch, "Charitable Foundations in the Sasanian Period" - Key article on the legal status of women and family structures.

Part 4 - War, Diplomacy, and Global Power

- Geoffrey Greatrex and Samuel Lieu, *The Roman Eastern Frontier and the Persian Wars, Part II: AD 363–630* (Routledge, 2002) - The essential sourcebook for the Roman-Persian wars; primary sources in translation with commentary. ★

- A.D.H. Bivar, "Cavalry Equipment and Tactics on the Euphrates Frontier" - Key article on Sasanian military organization.

- Étienne de la Vaissière, *Sogdian Traders: A History* (Brill, 2005) - Indispensable for understanding the Silk Road networks the Sasanians sat astride.

- Xinru Liu, *The Silk Road in World History* (Oxford University Press, 2010) - Accessible overview of the global trade networks connecting Persia to China and India. ★

Part 5 - Culture and Civilization

- Prudence Harper, *In Search of a Cultural Identity: Monuments and Artifacts of the Sasanian Near East* (Bibliotheca Persica, 2006) - The standard work on Sasanian material culture and art.

- Robert Hillenbrand (ed.), *The Art of the Sasanians* - Comprehensive survey of architecture, silverwork, and rock reliefs.

- Guitty Azarpay, *Sogdian Painting: The Pictorial Epic in Oriental Art* - Useful for understanding the artistic connections between Sasanian Persia and Central Asia.

- Kevin van Bladel, *The Arabic Hermes: From Pagan Sage to Prophet of Science* (Oxford University Press, 2009) - Essential for Chapter 18 on the translation movement and Gondeshapur.

- David Pingree, "The Logical Basis of Astrology in the Sasanian Period" - Key article on Sasanian contributions to astronomy and mathematics.

Part 6 - Crisis, Collapse, and Legacy

- James Howard-Johnston, *Witnesses to a World Crisis: Historians and Histories of the Middle East in the Seventh Century* (Oxford University Press, 2010) - The best scholarly analysis of the sources for the seventh-century collapse and Arab conquests. ★

- Fred Donner, *Muhammad and the Believers: At the Origins of Islam* (Harvard University Press, 2010) - Provides essential context for understanding the Arab conquests from the Islamic side. ★

- Patricia Crone, *Slaves on Horses: The Evolution of the Islamic Polity* (Cambridge University Press, 1980) - Classic study of how Islamic administration absorbed and adapted Sasanian administrative traditions.

- Parvaneh Pourshariati, *Decline and Fall of the Sasanian Empire* (I.B. Tauris, 2008) - The most detailed recent scholarly account of the empire's collapse; argues for the central role of the Parthian nobility. Essential reading for Chapters 19–21.

Key Journals and Online Resources

- **Encyclopaedia Iranica** (iranicaonline.org) - Free, peer-reviewed, continuously updated. The first stop for any topic related to Iranian history and culture.

- *Iran* - Journal of the British Institute of Persian Studies; the leading English-language journal for Sasanian studies.

- *Iranica Antiqua* - Belgian journal covering pre-Islamic Iranian history and archaeology; open access for older volumes.

- ***Journal of the Royal Asiatic Society*** - Regularly publishes articles on late antique Persia and adjacent topics.

- **Sasanika Project** (sasanika.org) - An academic project at UC Santa Barbara dedicated to Sasanian studies; publishes translations of Middle Persian inscriptions and accessible scholarly articles. Free online.